NEW NORDIC MEETS OLD ITALIAN

PERFECTLY PAIRED 45 VEGAN PASTA SAUCES

NEW NORDIC MEETS OLD ITALIAN

PERFECTLY PAIRED 45 VEGAN PASTA SAUCES

NEW NORDIC MEETS OLD ITALIAN

CONTENT

ABOUT THIS BOOK

"New Nordic Cuisine" is an innovative movement sweeps Scandinavia by combining little known local ingredients with a strong focus on health and an ethical production philosophy, modern techniques and playful vision. It has been used to promote local, natural and seasonal produce as a basis for new dishes both in restaurants and home.

Modern plant based nordic cooking can be applied to traditional Italian dishes easily.
There are unexpected similarities between Italian cooking and the New Nordic style; both kitchens make a cult of freshness, the seasons and simplicity.

Nordics always consider seasonal local and sustainable food like Italians; purity, freshness, simplicity and ethics, are aimed at bringing out the pure original flavours.

Scandinavian food is simple. When you work with the very best produce, there's no need to over complicate it. We call it husmanskost – farmer's fare. It's natural and honest, made with the staple produce found on the land.

Besides creative touches to the traditional recipes and little vegan cheese recipes to elevate your dishes, you will also find some gastronomic encounters between Italy and Sweden. I tried to convey more vividly by gourmet plates such as marinated beluga in glögg (Sweden's festive beverage - a kind of mulled wine) served with spaghetti and celeriac sauce. It is just fantastic with distinctly different levels of spicy sweetness of glögg with cherris and an earthy dish of celery.

This book also focuses on gourmet pasta sauces with unfamiliar edible plants that are prepared based on Italian cooking traditions, perfectly paired with dried pasta shapes.

The aim of this book is to encourage chefs to create a delicious plant based pasta menu in using 100% plants in the kitchen. There is a great range of unfamiliar plants that grow in every climate, though many of them are still unexplored in their culinary potential.

I heartly believe that ""New Nordic Meets Old Italian" will assist you to raise awareness about the tastes their environment offers and will allow to see them through different eyes.

Nazli Develi

NEW NORDIC MEETS OLD ITALIAN
Plant Based Chef & Author

THE BEST FOOD DOESN'T COME FROM THE BEST COOKS; THE BEST FOOD
COMES FROM THE BEST PEOPLE. PEOPLE WHO LOVE TO EAT.

PASTA PANTRY

To make any pasta recipe on the regular, here are some ideas for key ingredients to have on hand:

ESSENTIALS	AROMATICS	ADD - ON'S
Dried High Quality Pasta in Varying Shapes	Carrot	Peas
Extra Virgin Olive Oil	Onion	Eggplants
Canned Tomatoes	Garlic	Oat Tofu
Fresh Tomatoes	Peppercorns	Jack Fruit
Tomato Paste	Celery	Tempeh
Chili Flakes	Artichoke	Morel Mushrooms
Blackpepper	Fennel	Porcini Mushrooms
Almonds	Bay Leaves	Chantarelles
Pine Nuts	Asparagus	Trumpet Mushrooms
Cashews	Tarragon	Walnut
Oats	Parsley	Pea Protein
Cauliflower	Thyme	Kale
High Quality Salt	Marjoram	Lentil
Sherry Wine	Elder	Potato
Vegstock	Sage	Butternut Squash
White Wine	Rosemary	Hemp Hearts
Red Wine	Licorice	Chestnut
Truffle Oil	Bilberry	Plums
Aquavit or Vodka	Swedish Whitebeam	Apples
Citrus	Silverweed	Kalamata Olives
	Wood Sorrel	Capers
	Lingon	Vegan Parmesan
	Mallow	Avocado
	Juniper	
	Saffron	
	Coriander	
	Nutmeg	
	Dill	
	Basil	
	Wood Sorrel	
	Mustard Greens	
	Dandelion Greens	
	Oyster Leaves	

COOK PASTA THE ITALIAN WAY

Match your pasta shape to the sauce

Before you start, make sure you have chosen right pasta and sauce. The key measures here are size and texture. The sauce that is chosen for the pasta should stick to it and catch chunkier pieces in nooks.

A classic example of pasta choice gone wrong can be found in what many consider among the most Italian of dishes: Spaghetti Bolognese. Traditionally, a 'ragù alla Bolognese' is served with a long, thick pasta like tagliatelle that the hearty sauce can really cling to. When you pair thin strands of spaghetti with a heavy, meaty sauce, you tend to end up with a lot of lonely sauce at the bottom of your pasta bowl.

Use enough water

To cook pasta properly, you need to use a large, deep pot filled with a lot of water. This prevents the water from becoming too starchy and ensures the pasta has enough room to cook without sticking to itself. The rule is 1 litre/quart water for every 100g pasta.

Add pasta at the right time

Only add your pasta when the water comes to a rolling boil.

Salt your water well

I was always taught to salt the water only once it reaches a boil, so to my knowledge this was the proper way. But wider reading tells me that Italy is firmly divided in this matter: Some argue that salting from the beginning makes the water boil quicker, while late-salters warn that it'll corrode your pot.

Since there's no hard evidence for either, I will carry on salting as I do, once the water reaches a boil—but whichever way you do it, the important thing here is that you do in fact salt it, as the sodium really brings unseasoned dry or fresh pasta to life.

Never add oil to pasta water. The pasta won't stick together when you stir it often as it cooks. Adding oil to the water will create a slippery surface on pasta and the sauce will adhere poorly to the pasta when it is time to combine the two.

Cook Al dente

Al dente means 'to the tooth' in Italian—a degree of cooking that ensures a little chew to your pasta and makes for a more interesting, textured final dish. To achieve this, try removing the pasta about 1 – 2 min. before the advised cooking time on the package, or simply scoop out a piece or two to test before draining.

Remember to cook pasta always for less than the cooking time, and it will remain hard. Go over the cooking time and it will become softer and softer and this is what we don't want.

Use your pasta water

Pasta water is integral to making virtually every pasta sauce, acting as a starchy base, thickener and helping to create a glossy finish. Add it to loosen things up as you toss your pasta with pesto, create the sauce for "cacio e pepe", to stretch out "aglio e olio" or to add life to a dry ragu. Before draining, I always reserve at least one big mug-full of pasta water to splash into the final dish little by little until I've reached my desired consistency.

Toss your pasta with the sauce before serving

Rather than topping cooked pasta with your chosen sauce, give your pasta a chance to really unite with the sauce by tossing it in as soon as you've drained it (but only after you've reserved your pasta water). Best way is to use a seperate pot for cooking sauce. The hotter starchy pasta will bind better with the sauce and absorb the flavor, creating a more well-rounded dish. Again, adding a little pasta water here helps it all come together.

'Mantecare' - Emulsion – How Italians making sauce actually cling to pasta

The act of skillfully combining cooked pasta with a sauce is something Italians call the 'mantecare'.
This literally means to emulsify the starch (loosen from the boiled pasta) with the oil in the sauce to make that creamy loose pasta finish that is so compelling.

An emulsion is a scientific concept that simply means at least two liquids that normally won't mix have been forced to come together. In the world of food, you might already recognize this concept in the difference between repellant oil and vinegar on the one hand, and a thick, creamy vinaigrette on the other. The latter, which somehow contains both oil and vinegar and yet doesn't seem to separate right away, is an emulsion.

There are absolutely vital steps to emulsifying any kind of pasta sauce: reserving some pasta water, introducing fat slowly.

Here are what you need for combining pasta and sauce:

A Large sauté pan, wide, deep, heavy-bottomed, long-handled and preferably non-stick
A cup of salty, starchy pasta cooking water
Extra virgin olive oil

How to mantecare?

1. Drain the pasta but keep a cup of the cooking water.
2. Tip the hot drained pasta into the pan containing the sauce, adding 50 ml of the cooking water.
3. Then toss together over a high heat until the pasta looks creamy and well coated.

REDUCTION TIPS

What is reduction?

Reduction is the process of thickening and intensifying the flavor of a liquid mixture such as a soup, sauce, wine, or juice by simmering.

One of the simplest ways to add flavor into your pastas and a more impressive presentation to your home cooking repertoire is to reduce liquid and pan drippings into lush, thick, spoon-coating sauces.

It´s a simple to to make reduction. But mastering the art of reducing sauce requires a little savviness.

Here´s how to fast track your sauce from simple to complex, silky, and spoonable:

1. Whatever solids are in your pan such as mushrooms, seitan, jack fruit or vegetables, they´re standing in the way of your braising liquid. Remove fully-cooked and tender mushrooms from the pan and let it rest while the sauce cooks over medium heat. Once the sauce has reached your desired consistency, add the mushrooms back in and rewarm it over gentle heat, spooning the sauce over.

2. The more surface area your sauce has to do its thing, the quicker it´ll reduce. A large dutch oven or wide sauté pan will yield the quickest results. The deeper the pan´s volume, the longer it´ll take to condense and reduce.

3. Keep the pot uncovered. Because the point of reducing liquid is to let it evaporate, you need to give that liquid access to the air.

4. A good reduction takes a fair amount of time, and it´s ideal to simmer, rather than boil. Too-high heat can cause the sauce to over-reduce and become bitter.

5. Once your liquid has reduced to the perfect consistency , whisk in a tablespoon extra virgin olive oil. It will give it a beautifully glossy sheen.

6. If you´ve dutifully followed steps but your sauce still hasn´t properly reduced you can hack it with a slurry. A slurry is simply a combination of starch mixed with liquid. Some classic slurries include: cornstarch, tapioca starch, arrowroot, potato starch, and water or vegstock.
When I add a slurry, I usually prefer to go with tapioca, vegetable or mushroom stock.

COMMON PASTA SAUCE FORMULA

This book includes some good recipes to inspire you. They are great place to start. But if you want to try your own pasta sauce, there is very simple formula to follow.

If you have some ingredients we've listed in the pantry chaptber, you will be able to start making your own pasta right away:

Aromatics : Onion, Garlic, Leek, Artichoke, Celery, Fennel...

Herbs & Spices: Pepper, Thyme, Basil, Sage, Dill, Tarragon, Rosemary...

Liquid: Mushroom Stock, Veg Stock, Almond Milk, Oat Cream, Coconut Cream etc..

Veggies: Tomato, Carrot, Zucchini, Broccoli, Beet...

Protein (optional) : Lentils, Beans, Quinoa, Hemp Seeds, Peanuts...

Meaty Stuff (optional): Mushrooms, Jack Fruit, Tofu, Seitan, Tempeh

Cheese: Nut Cheeses, Nutritional Yeast, Cashews, Sunflower Seeds

Toppings: Cashews Parmesan, Basil, Microgreens, Sprouts Edible Flowers, Toasted Fruits etc..

How to

1. Gather your ingredients, cut and chop as needed, then add to the pot. Cook stirring occasionally. This is quick way to make your own sauce.

2. Bring to boil over high heat and reduce the heat to low and simmer stirring occasionally until bubbled. Toss with your pasta and top with toppings, enjoy.

Serving Size

For Pasta Secca (dry pasta)
- 100g uncooked pasta per person as a one-course meal
- 70-80g uncooked pasta per person as an appetizer
- 50g uncooked pasta per person when added to soups

For Pasta Fresca (fresh pasta)
- 80g uncooked pasta per person as a one-course meal
- 30-40g uncooked fresh pasta per person when added to soups.

Choosing High Quality Italian Pasta

Have you ever noticed that little sliver of your grocery store's pasta section that just looks better? The brands aren't instantly recognizable. The logos seem like they were hand-drawn with a large quill pen or stamped with an antique letterpress. And the prices, well, they're definitely a bit higher than the typical dried stuff you've been buying. But I just want to say that, by and large, that expensive pasta is worth the extra cash. At the end, by means of both satisfying your soul and stomach, it is definitely worth more.

But why? Isn't dried pasta all the same?
Here's why the pricier stuff is totally worth it.

The first reason is a low-temperature, slow-drying process. When we're talking about good dried pasta, this is probably the most important thing.

Most (industrial) dried pasta brands will dry their pasta at higher temperature, so it loses moisture more quickly. This gives them the ability to make more pasta, more quickly, which means they can produce and sell more. This quick-drying process traps undeveloped starch proteins inside the dried pasta. What that really means is that the texture of quick-dried pasta is inferior to that of slow-dried.

Cheap pasta is also made with thin flour, it softens very quickly and it is hard to cook al dante. You won't feel full when you eat. It just inflates your stomach.

You can understand this by looking at the pasta itself. If the pasta looks shiny and smooth, it's not going to be that great at absorbing sauce.

If the pasta looks kind of rough, chalky, and a little dirty, that's a great sign. Sauce loves to cling to that bumpy exterior texture. And if the outside looks a little worn, it's probably a sign that the pasta was shaped using bronze dies. (A die is just another word for pasta mold.)

Slow-dried pasta is more pleasant to eat at a perfect al dente—toothy, chewy, and delicious. It takes a longer amount of time to slow-dry pasta, which is one half of the reason it's more expensive.

PAIRING PASTA SHAPES WITH SAUCES

Do you know that there are over 300 types of pasta shapes?

And as we unconditionally love pasta, we are firmly convinced that there is good reason for pasta to exist in so many forms! First and foremost: Choosing the right pasta shape to compliment your sauce or accompaniments makes a big difference to your finished dish.

Some pasta types are best eaten with a certain set of ingredients, while others work well with a wide variety of sauces. Generally, larger shapes work better with thick, rich sauces, while skinny, more delicate shapes suit lighter sauces.

Italians have spent centuries developing pasta shapes to catch, trap or elude their saucy counterparts. The general rule is long smooth shapes for oily sauces (spaghetti, linguine, tagliatelle) where you do not want to trap the oil. Cleaver sauce-catching shapes and wide fresh pastas to catch all the flavour of hearty toma-to-based sauces (shells, rigatoni, fusilli, farfelle). It is worth noting that each shape, size and type will have a different optimum cooking time.

For a light cream sauce (almond, cauliflower, cashew or oat based) : Lighter sauces are great with longer-style noodles like fettuccine or spaghetti. They carry the sauce well and add some good texture to counteract the thin and smooth sauce.

For a tomato-based sauce: Long, thin shapes are great here. The sauce pairs well with shapes such as spaghetti, linguine, or angel hair, and binds well with the thin noodle.

For a vegetable-based sauce such as pesto, broccoli, peas: Orecchiette, both smaller and larger cup sizes, are good to use with this kind of sauce. Fusilli, cavatappi, and rotini are also good. They lend themselves to a good texture on the palate and hold the sauce well so you get a perfect bite on the spoon.

For mushroom/jack or lentil bolognese: The meaty chunks in these sauces are easily mopped up by tube-shaped pastas like penne, bucatini, tubini, and tortiglioni. "The chunks can enter the tubes and the pasta acts as a great vehicle to carry the sauce.

A LITTLE REGIONAL GUIDE TO ITALIAN PASTA

The big variety of types of pasta comes from the different culinary traditions in the different regions. In the Italian national cuisine there are different types of pasta from the same or neighboring regions that have made their reputation.

The many types of pasta can be confusing to foreigners but Italians and culinary experts know that it's about specific rules. Sauces also have their specifics according to the region.

Today, spaghetti must have an exactly specific size: long between 35 and 40 cm and the section – between 0.7 and 0.09 mm. Everything else is another type of pasta. For example, spaghettini which are thinner and combine with lighter types of sauce and spices.

Most researchers point to Genoa as the homeland of classic spaghetti, although over time they have moved towards Naples and it has "seized the functions" as a homeland.

Nowadays there is a traditional Spaghetti Celebration in Naples where there are 10% of the Italian pasta makers, with about 3 million tons of pasta per year and exportation to all continents.

Fettuccine are typical of Bologna; hard wheat is used for their making. These are flat and wide rolled bands. Here they were also inspired by the legend of Venus' navel.

Fusili with their specific spiral shape come from the region of Naples and there is a shorter and a longer variant. This kind of pasta is served with more liquid types of sauce.

The Emilia-Romagna region is represented by garganelli – the only pasta in the shape of a tube made by hand.

Sicily has artistically enlisted with the wheels – a type of pasta which is a peculiar model of cart wheels.

There are also different types of sauce. Tomato sauces are most common in Southern Italy where they are prepared in a spicier manner by adding garlic and hot spices. In Northern Italy most common types are the softer white sauces based on cream.

Tuscany

In the northwest of the peninsula, Tuscany is one of the most popular regions of Italy for it's wineries, rolling hills, and, of course, food. Keeping it simple is one of the skills of Tuscan cuisine, and results of quality over quantity speak for themselves. Take the ricotta and spinach gnudi for example. It takes just a handful of ingredients to make these impressively pillowy Tuscan dumplings that, while they aren't exactly pasta, seems to straddle the line right along with another Italian favorite: gnocchi.

Puglia

Puglia might not be the best known region of Italy when it comes to cuisine, but as the home of burrata and orecchiette, Puglia is certainly still represented. In this southern region that boasts hundreds of miles of shoreline from both the Adriatic and Ionian seas, the number one pasta is orecchiette dressed with bitter greens. (See "orecchiette with spirulina matcha cream and bitter oyster leaves" in this book) Another way to enjoy these little ear-shaped pastas? A creamy rendition with radicchio and walnuts, pesto or tomatoes.

Campania

Near the tip of the boot, Campania is a southwestern region of Italy that might be equally known for its dramatic coastlines (see Amalfi Coast, Mount Vesuvius, etc.) as it is for the arguably world-famous Neapolitan cuisine. From pizza Margherita to the shell-shaped sfogliatella pastry, pasta e fagioli (pasta with beans) to pasta puttanesca, the cuisine of Campania varies depending on where you are in the region, but you're likely to run into variations on these two classic Campanian pastas no matter where you end up.

Emilia-Romagna

A region in northeastern Italy, the capital of Emilia-Romagna is Bologna—home to the world's oldest university and the much-loved meat sauce, ragú Bolognese. While this wealthy region is tied to many other well-known recipes and culinary traditions—from balsamic vinegar to Parmigiano Reggiano—for us, Bolognese takes the gold medal. When you take the time and make the effort to recreate the vegan version of Bolognese, we think you'll agree.

Lazio

Housing the country's capital, Lazio is the second most populated region in Italy. Located on the western side near the center of the peninsula, the region is to thank for our favorite, creamy pasta dish: cacio e pepe or a spicy tomato dish : penne all'arrabbiata.

Liguria

A small, curved crescent along the northwestern coast of Italy, Liguria is often referred to as the Italian riviera—a popular tourist destination with picturesque cliffside towns and sandy beaches. Pesto originates from Liguria, so you can just as sure that like the aquamarine sea meets the terracotta-roofed houses at the shore, pesto meets plenty of plates of pasta in Liguria.

Sicily

Though Sicily, the largest island in the Mediterranean, is today an autonomous region of Italy, it has a long history of switching hands—from the Greeks to the Arabs. Each region of the island itself is known for something special, say, sweets like cannoli or granita, and influences from its history come through in various ways from the use of certain spices to preferences over seafood. That being said, dishes like this seafood pasta, pasta alla norma (with macaroni, tomatoes, fried aubergines, grated ricotta salata cheese, and basil.) and arancini (fried rice balls)—are found in their different forms throughout the island.

NUT CHEESES TO ELEVATE YOUR PASTA

Almond Ricotta

Ingredients

250 g. slivered blanched almonds (can be made with cashews or macadamia as well)

2 tbsp nutritional yeast

2 tbsp lemon juice

1 tsp garlic powder

1 tsp salt

1 tbsp marjoram

Directions

1. Soak the almonds in hot water for at least an hour. In a blender- add the almonds and all of the soaking liquid. Puree the almonds and the soaking water on high until smooth. Season to taste with salt.

2. Line a fine strainer with a few layers of cheese cloth and position the strainer over a large bowl.

3. Strain the almond milk into the cheese cloth and let drip for about 30 minutes. Collect all of the almond milk. Now wrap the almond solids up tightly in the cheesecloth, forming it into a ball.

4. Place it in a clean bowl in the refrigerator and let firm up for at least a few hours before you unwrap the ball.

5. Drizzle of olive oil and a sprinkle of red pepper flakes or fresh marjoram.

At this point, the "ricotta" is ready to enjoy, especially in dishes like lasagna or stuffed pasta shells. However, it can also be wrapped in cheesecloth, formed into a ball, and placed into a fine mesh strainer set over a mixing bowl up to 3 days. This will allow the ricotta to firm up a bit.

Cultured Macadamia

Ingredients

220 g. raw macadamia nuts

4 g. acidophilus probiotic

1/3 cup filtered water

2 tbsp nutritional yeast

2 tbsp lemon juice

1/4 tsp sea salt

1/2 bunch fresh dill to coat

Directions

1. Place nuts in a jar. Cover with filtered warm water and close the lid. Let it rest in the room temperature at least 1 hour. Then place in the fridge for 6 hours. This process will activate the nuts and also yields a neutral nut flavor.

2. Dissolve probiotic powder in a little water, set aside.

3. Set 6 tbsp water nut aside. Strain and rinse nuts.

4. Place 6 tbsp of water, strained nuts and dissolved probiotic into the food processor. Mix on high speed until smooth.

5. Transfer mixture to a nut milk bag. Gather up the ends to create a ball. Wrap the ends and squeeze out any excess moisture.

6. Place cheese in the dehydrator at 30° C for about 20-24 hours to let it ferment. House with an average temperature of 25-30° C four 24 hours.

7. Once fermentation time is up, open the cheesecloth and observe your cheese carefully. You will notice a yellowish crust formed on top. That is totally normal. If there is pink or bluish spots, it indicates the presence of mold; throw away the cheese and restart.

8. If everything is ok, transfer cheese from its cloth to a bowl and stir in nutritional yeast, lemon juice, and salt. You can also add in other flavours whatever you like.

9. Form a log or ball on a piece of parchment paper and place in the refrigerator overnight.

10. Last step is rolling in a salty herby mixture. On a flat surface, spread out chopped fresh dill and sprinkle some salt.

Aged Almond Pepper Jack

200g almonds (soaked & blanced overnight)

4g acidophilus probiotic

4-5 tbsp filtered water

3 tbsp nutritinal yeast

4-5 sun dried tomatoes & red bell pepper

1 tbsp lemon juice

1 tsp licorice salt (I use saltverk brand, it is unique one)

smoked paprika for coating

Directions:

1. Make the cheese according to cultured macadamia recipe on the page 18.

2. Just add sundried tomatoes , red bell pepper & nutritional yeast when you are on the step 4 and blend them well in the food processor. Follow the process. Once it is done, coat with paprika and licorice salt.

3. As you can consume the cheese next day, you can leave it to fermente for a week. The cheese will lose some water day by day, pat it dry with a paper towel if it is too wet and replace the parchment paper with new one. For the 2 next weeks, flip the cheese everyday and change the parchment paper regulary if it becomes wet. At the end cover with smoked paprika and licorice salt. Keep in the refrigerator.

Vegan Butter

Cultured Milk

70 g. raw macadamia soaked

150 g. water

1 capsule acidophilus (or a pinch of mesophilic culture)

Cultured Butter

1/2 cup cultured cashew milk

220 g. refined coconut oil

60 g. grapeseed oil

1/8 tsp turmeric powder for color

1/4 tsp salt

Directions:

1. Add soaked nuts to a blender with the 2/3 cup water and blend on high speed until smooth. Scrape down the sides from time to time until everything is smooth.

2. Transfer to a small bowl and stir in the acidophilus powder. Cover with a clean towel and let sit at room temperature for at least 24 hours. It should have a light sour taste, and you should see some air bubbles.

3. Melt the coconut oil over low-medium heat. Measure 1 and 1/4 cup of melted coconut oil and put it in a blender. Add 1/2 cup of cultured macadamia milk, grapeseed oil, , salt, and turmeric. Blend on high speed about 1 minute.

4. Line a small pan with parchment paper. Transfer the mixture to the container and place in the freezer at least 1 hour, or until firm.

5. Once firm, transfer to the refrigerator. It will become softer after a few hours.

It will keep for up to 7 days in the refrigerator.

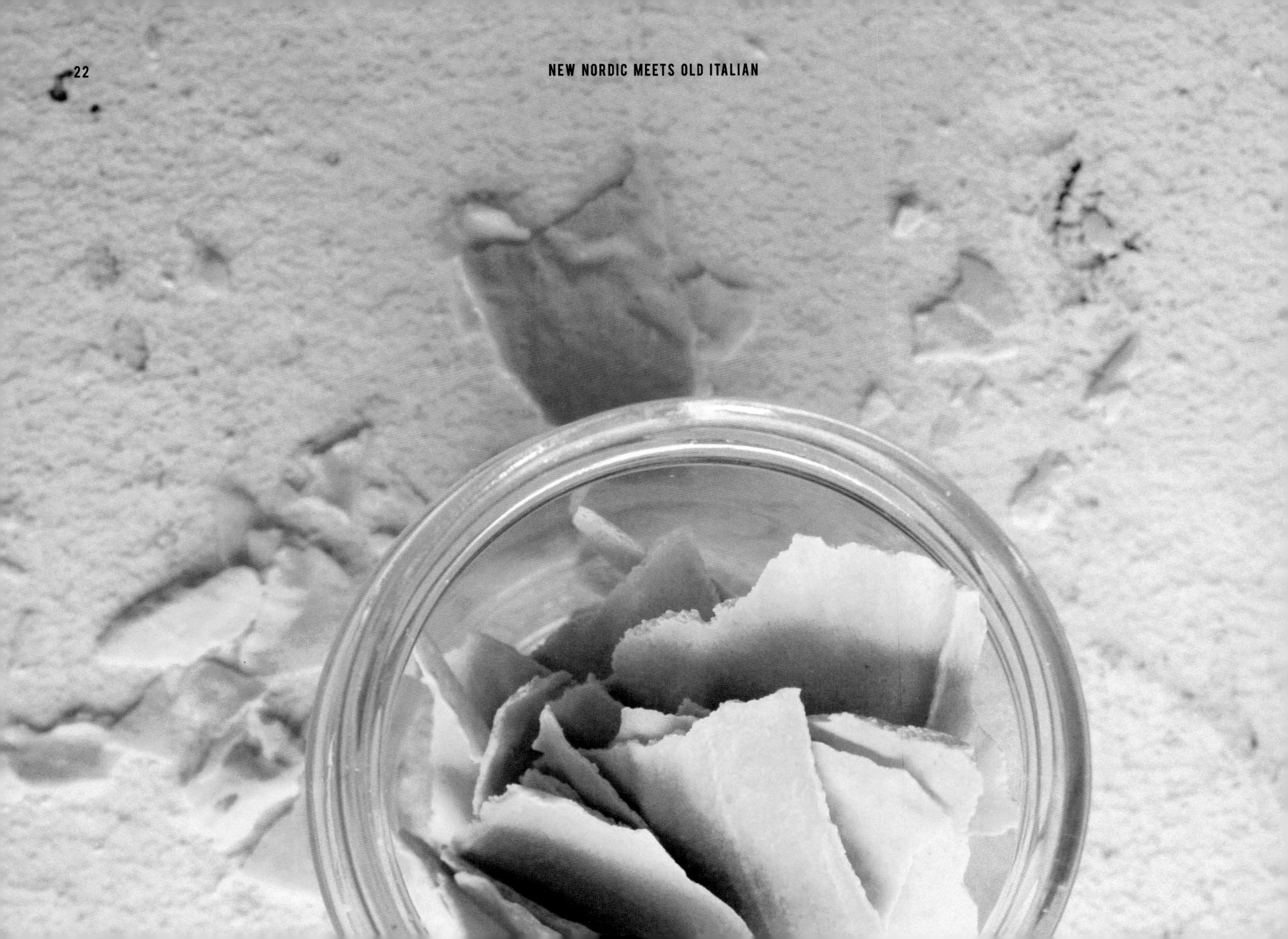

Dehydrated Sunflower Parmesan Flakes

Ingredients:

140 g. sunflower or cashew (alternative almond and sunflower seeds can be mixed together)

5 tablespoons of nutritional yeast (nutritional yeast)

3 tablespoons of lemon juice

1 teaspoon of tamari (or miso)

1 tablespoon of apple cider vinegar

A pinch of turmeric powder

1/8 teaspoon red pepper (optional)

1/2 teaspoon pink Himalayan salt

1/2 teaspoon mushroom powder (optional preferably porcini, portobello or shiitake)

1/2 teaspoon garlic powder

5 tablespoons of water

Method:

1. Soak the nuts in the water for 2-3 hours, then rinse and drain, transfer to the blendtec twister jar.

2. Add the remaining ingredients to the blender. Mix at high speed until you get a smooth mixture.

3. Place a non-stick paper to a dehydrator tray. Spread the cheese mixture very thinly using offset spatula.

4. Bake it in the dehydrator at 42 ° C for about 10-12 hours.

5. After 6 hours, flip the cheese using a new dehydrator paper, transfer to a new paper. Then cook back side of the cheese for another 6 hours.

6. When your cheese is baked, cut it into small pieces and keep it in the jar.

Easy Powder Cashew Parmesan

150 g cashews

4 tbsp nutritional yeast

1 tsp salt

1/4 tsp dried lemon powder

Method:

Add everything to a blender and mix until finely ground. If you prefer, you can also leave some bigger chunks in it by pulsing until it's combined but not finely ground.

NORDIC ITALIAN FUSION

SPAGHETTI WITH GLÖGG MARINATED BELUGA & CELERIAC

A TASTE OF NORTHERN ISLAND

TAGLIATELLE WITH SWEDISH MEATBALLS & LINGON

RIGATONI DI LAPLAND

BLUE CASARECCE WITH TRUMPET & BLUEBERRIES

SPAGHETTI WITH CABBAGE & MUSTARD

CONCHIGLIE RIGATE ALFREDO WITH DANDELION GREENS

SPAGHETTI WITH LICORICE CHANTERELLES

CASARECCE CARAMELIZED PORCINI & BALSAMIC

LINGUINE WITH CHOCOLATE AND NORDIC BERRIES

GNOCCHI PASTA WITH SKAGENRÖRA

NEW NORDIC MEETS OLD ITALIAN

SPAGHETTI WITH GLOGG MARINATED BELUGA & CELERIAC

MARINATED BELUGA

Beluga Lentils	65	G
Glögg	2	DL
Water	1	DL
Olive Oil	2	TBSP
Salt	1	TSP

DECORATION

Fresh thyme, halved fresh cherries, vegan parmesan

APPLE CELERY PUREE

Carrot	45	G
Celery Root	100	G
Onion	50	G
Red Apple	100	G
Olive Oil	2	TBSP
Salt	1	TSP
Fresh Thyme	1	SPRING
Nutritional Yeast	1	TBSP
Lime Juice	1	TBSP

DIRECTIONS

1. Add the glögg to a container with the cooked beluga and let it sit in the fridge for 12 hours.
2. Once the time is up, strain lentils, set aside.
3. Transfer glögg sauce you strained to a pan. Reduce over a medium-high heat until thick. Set aside.
4. Add a dash of oil to a large pan, place over a high heat and add the beluga lentils, searing all over until a deep golden brown colour. Season with salt once browned and remove from the pan. Set aside.
5. Add another dash of oil to a different pan and add the carrot, celery, apple and onion. Cover with water. Cook until soft but without colour, then add some fresh thyme.
6. When soften, transfer to a blender with a pinch of salt, nutritional yeast, lime juice and water if you need.. Blitz to a very smooth purée, adjusting the consistency with a little of the agave syrup, if necessary. Set aside.
7. Transfer mixture in a saucepan, cook until bubbled. Then pour in a deep plate.
8. Add your cooked pasta into glögg sauce, drizzle olive oil and salt, toss well.
9. Transfer into plate giving it a moon shape on the sauce.
10. Top with beluga lentils.
11. Decorate with fresh thyme and halved cherries. Serve with vegan parmesan.

NEW NORDIC MEETS OLD ITALIAN

A TASTE OF NORTHERN ISLAND

INGREDIENTS ————

Cashews or Macadamia soaked	80 G
Nutritional Yeast	2 TBSP
Olive Oil	2-3 TBSP
Butterfly Pea Flower Powder	1/2 TSP
Gangnam Tops, Maji Leaves	4-5 LEAVES
Lemon Juice	2 TBSP
Sea Fennel	3-4 SPRING
Crispy Kale	2 LARGE LEAVES
Fresh Bilberries	5-6 TBSP
Silver Powder	1 TSP
Nasturtium leaves (optional)	4-5
Zallotti Blossom	TO DECORATE
Salt & Pepper	TO TASTE

DIRECTIONS

Prepare your sauce simultaneously to avoid overcooking the pasta while at rest.

1- Cook the pasta al dante, set aside 1 cup pasta water to use for the sauce. Toss pasta with a tablespoon olive oil and sprinkle some salt. Set aside.

2. In a high speed blender, add soaked cashews, lemon juice, nutritional yeast, 1/2 tsp salt, butterfly pea flower powder and 100ml pasta water. Mix on high speed until silky smooth.

3. Transfer mixture in a pot, add 1 tbsp olive oil. Cook on low heat until bubbled. Add more pasta water and olive oil if you need to thin sauce.

4. In a large saute pan, heat 1 tbsp olive oil, add 2-3 large kale leaves. Fry until crispy, set aside.

5. Coat fresh bilberries with silver powder, set aside.

6. When the sauce is done, pour in a deep large plate. Place a large crispy kale leaf in the right side of plate.

7. Add shell pasta on the leaf.

8. Add bilberry pearls in the shells.

9. Lightly toss sea fennel and maji leaves in olive oil. Add to your plate.

10. Decorate with gangnam tops and zallotti blossoms.

TAGLIATELLE WITH SWEDISH MEATBALLS & LINGON

VEGAN SWEDISH MEATBALLS

Roasted Cauliflower	130 G
Cooked Quinoa	130 G
Flaxseed Eggs	2
Red Onion diced	100 G
Black Pepper	1/2 TSP
Garlic Cloves	5 LARGE
Breadcrumbs GF*	140 G
Red Chili Flakes	1/2 TSP
Salt	1 TSP
Olive Oil	2 TBSP

WHITE SAUCE

Vegan Butter	3 TBSP
Oat Flour	130 G
Vegetable Broth	2 CUPS
Oat Cream	250 ML
Tamari**	2 TBSP
Dijon Mustard	1/2 TSP
BlackPepper	140 G
Red Chili Flakes	1/4 TSP
Parsley	3 TBSP
Salt	TO TASTE

DIRECTIONS

VEGAN SWEDISH MEATBALLS

1. Preheat oven to 220°C. Cut the cauliflower's stem off, and cut into even-sized florets. Drizzle the cauliflower with a teaspoon of oil. Roast the cauliflower for 15 minutes in the oven. Remove and allow to cool for a few minutes.

2. In a food processor, add the cauliflower and pulse it until it's completely riced. Remove from the food processor. You only need 1 cup of this for this recipe and 8 ounces (~226 gram) should make about 1 cup.

3. Add the 1 cup of riced cauliflower and all the other meatball ingredients. You can pulse them or mix them together until they form into a tight ball, combining everything. You want to ensure they are so mixed together that you're not seeing individual cauliflower or quinoa florets, it's all one big mixture. That's how you'll ensure the meatballs will hold together.

4. Heat the olive oil in a pan over medium high heat. While it's heating, use a tablespoon measurer to form one raw meatball and shape into a ball with your fingers. You can place them on a plate while the oil heats.

5. Add one meatball to test the oil. Cook on one side for about 1-2 minutes, turning on all sides onto fully cooked inside and out, about 4 minutes. You can add as many meatballs as can fit in the pan without overcrowding it, cooking them all for about 4-5 minutes turning on each side, to cook them through.

6. Turn the heat off. Prep the sauce either in this cooled down pan, or in a separate pan then add the meatballs to it as in the sauce directions.

*Gluten-free

** Start with 1 tablespoon tamari , add more if you think you need it. Also, if you don't use light soy sauce or tamari, please note that it will be saltier, so adjust the salt accordingly.

WHITE SAUCE

1. In a pan over medium heat, melt the vegan butter. Add the oat flour to a pan, and whisk vigorously with a whisk until the flour is fully incorporated with the butter with no lumps, forming a roux. Let it cook for about 2 minutes to remove any flour taste.

2. Slowly mix in the vegetable broth, whisking at the same time, until a smooth sauce is formed. Add in the can of oat cuisine cream , whisking at the same time too until fully incorporated.

3. Add in the tamari, mustard, black pepper and 1 tablespoon of the parsley. Mix, taste, and add salt to test.

4. Remove the sauce from the heat and add in the meatballs, slowly turning to coat the meatballs. Add the last of the parsley to garnish and serve with pasta and lingonberries.

NEW NORDIC MEETS OLD ITALIAN

RIGATONI DI LAPLAND

This recipe is colourful fusion of Italian and Northern influences. The fragrant blend of kale, basil and peas creates an unusual pesto recipe you'll find yourself turning to again and again, it has a striking and unusual flavour of its own. Served with a blended purple sauce, crispy morel, a sprinkling of olive oil and snowed vegan parmesan this is a wonderfully intricate pasta starter.

KALE PESTO

Kale Leaves	50 G + MORE FOR GARNISH
Walnuts	20 G
Fresh Basil	25 G
Garlic Cloves	1/2
Olive Oil	4 TBSP
Peas	40 G
Nutritional Yeast	1 TBSP
Salt	1 TSP
Onion Petals	FROM 1 ONION
Water	3-4 TBSP

PURPLE SAUCE

Purple Potato	50 G
Red Onion	1 SMALL
Lemon Juice	1 TBSP
Almond Milk	4 TBSP
Salt	1 TSP
Olive Oil	2 TBSP
Morel Mushrooms	30 G
Silver Powder	TO BRUSH MORELS

DIRECTIONS

1. If using dried morel mushrooms, place them in a bowl and cover with warm water to rehydrate. Once soft, drain and rinse well, set aside.

2. To make kale pesto, Place everything except the oil and pea in a food processor. Blend briefly to combine, then gradually add the oil -- blending continuously -- until fully incorporated.

3. Add the peas and pulse very briefly until just combined with the pesto, leaving a chunky texture. Set aside until ready to serve.

4. In a large pan, heat olive oil, add onions and cook until soften.

5. Boil your purple potato until soften well.

6. Transfer onions and purple potato into your blender, add lemon juice, salt, olive oil and almond milk. Blend well until smooth. If it is too thick then add more almond milk or just water. Transfer to a pipping bag. Set aside.

7. Meanwhile, place the morel mushrooms in a frying pan and cook over a high heat until crisp, then sprinkle some salt.. Drain any excess oil on kitchen paper. Then brush some silver powder. Set aside.

8. Brush the kale leaves with a little oil and fry for 30 seconds in the pan with a little olive oil until the leaves are crisp. Season with a little salt.

9. To serve, place purple potato sauce in a pipping bag, decorate creating dots on the plate. Heat kale pesto with a little pasta water until bubbled. Then toss the kale pesto through the cooked pasta and divide between the plates, making a small pile or stack as you see in the picture.

10. Scatter the red onion petals and fried morels around the plate, topping with the crisp kale leaves. Garnish with some of the olive oil powder and a sprinkling of vegan parmesan.

BLUE CASARECCE WITH TRUMPET & BLUEBERRIES

TRUMPET MUSHROOMS

Trumpet Mushrooms	40 G
Red onion	12-14
Garlic	4 CLOVES
Salt	1/2 TSP
Pasta Water	1/2 CUP
Olive oil	2 TBSP

BLUEBERRIES

Blueberries	3 TBSP
Lemon Juice	130 G
Silver Powder	2 CUPS

BLUE PASTA

Butterfly Pea Powder	1 TSP
Pasta Water	1/2 CUP
Olive Oil	1 TBSP
Salt	1/2 TSP

DIRECTIONS

1. Soak dried trumpet mushrooms or brush well if you are using fresh mushrooms.

2. Cut into small pieces. Add to a large hot pan with olive oil. Add chopped onions and garlic. Fry them in a hot pan on high heat for 3-4 minutes. Salt to taste. We want them very crispy. So if they look soft, continue cooking for 2-3 minutes.

3. Wash and strain blueberries and place in a small pan, add 1 tbsp lemon juice. Cook on low heat until puffy. Then remove from the heat. Set aside.

4. In a pot, add 1 tbsp olive oil, 1/2 cup pasta water, salt and butterfly pea flower powder. Mix well. Cook on medium heat until bubbled.

5. Then toss with your pasta on high heat for 20-30 seconds.

6. Divide between plates. Add mushrooms on top.

7. Cover blueberries with silver powder to make them shiny if desired and add to the plate.

8. Serve with vegan parmesan if desired.

* Gluten-free.

** Start with 1 tablespoon tamari , add more if you think you need it. Also, if you don't use light soy sauce or tamari, please note that it will be saltier, so adjust the salt accordingly.

NEW NORDIC MEETS OLD ITALIAN

SPAGHETTI WITH CABBAGE & MUSTARD SAUCE

INGREDIENTS ——————

White Cabbage	1/4 HEAD
GF Nutritional Yeast	4 TBSP
Garlic Cloves	4-5
Extra Virgin Olive Oil	3-4 TBSP
Salt	1 TSP
Vegan Parmesan	2 TBSP
Red Chili Flakes	TO SERVE
Mustard	3 TBSP
Capers	TO SERVE

DIRECTIONS

1. Cut the cabbage in half and, with the cut-side down, slice it as thinly as possible around the core, as though you were making coleslaw. Discard the core.

2. Heat 1 tbsp olive oil in a large saute pan or heavy-bottomed pot over medium-high heat. Add the cabbage, salt, and pepper and saute for 8 to 10 minutes, stirring occasionally, until the cabbage is tender and begins to brown. Then remove the heat. Set aside.

3. In a small bowl, combine salt, mustard, lemon juice and olive oil. Whisk together to form the dressing. Set aside 2 tbsp dressing to top later. Pour the remaining dressing over cabbage, mix well.

4. Add your cooked spaghetti in the saute pan. Toss with cabbage.

5. Divide pasta between plates. Pour mustard sauce on top. Sprinkle some chili peppers and vegan parmesan.

6. Decorate with capers and serve immediately.

NEW NORDIC MEETS OLD ITALIAN

CONCHIGLIE RIGATE ALFREDO WITH DANDELION GREENS

INGREDIENTS

Cauliflower Florets	160 G
Dandelion Greens	1 CUP
Nutritional Yeast	1 TBSP
Tamari	1 TBSP
Onion	1 MEDIUM
Garlic Cloves	2-3
Pasta Water	1.5 CUP
Olive Oil	3 TBSP
Salt	1 TSP
Bay Leaves	2
Chili Pepper	1/4 TSP
Peas	2-3 TBSP

DIRECTIONS

1. Heat the oil in a medium-sized pot over medium-high heat. Add the onion and let it cook for 3-4 minutes until soft.

2. Add chopped garlic and red pepper flakes , cook until golden brown. Add the cauliflower and 1 cup pasta water to the pot, cover with a lid and let the cauliflower steam for 5 minutes, or until you can pierce it easily with a fork.

3. Transfer the cauliflower , add 1/2 cup pasta water and other pot contents to a blender and blend until smooth. Add the remaining ingredients (starting with 1 tablespoon of nutritional yeast , tamari and 1 teaspoon of salt) and blend again. Taste and add more nutritional yeast and sea salt, if you'd like. Transfer mixture in a pot, add bay leaves, cook on low heat for 5-6 minutes. Then remove bay leaves.

4. Use sauce right away or store it in a glass mason jar until you are ready to use it. When ready, pour sauce into a pan to keep warm. Toss with pasta when ready and serve immediately.

5. When you are ready to serve your pasta, add the dandelion greens to the skillet and cook, stirring, until wilted, 1 to 2 minutes. Stir in the cauliflower alfredo and season to taste with salt and pepper. Keep warm over low heat.

6. Serve with some peas if you like.

SPAGHETTI WITH LICORICE CHANTERELLES

INGREDIENTS

Chanterelles*	12
Juniper** or Lingonberries	12-14
Licorice Salt of Saltverk	A PINCH
Olive Oil	3 TBSP
Wood Sorrel or Parsley	1/2 BUNCH
Tomato Paste	1 TBSP
Garlic Cloves sliced	4
Himalayan Salt	1 TSP

DIRECTIONS

1. Soak the juniper or lingonberries.
2. Fry the chantarelles in a hot pan on high heat for 3-4 minutes with 1 tbsp of olive oil. Licorice salt to taste. We want them very crispy. So if they look soft, continue cooking for 2-3 minutes until get brown.
3. Strain berries and place in a small pan, add 1 tbsp chia seeds. Cook on low heat until you get jelly-like form. Then remove from the heat. Transfer mixture a pipping bag and set it in the refrigerator while you are making pasta.
4. In a pot, add 2 tbsp olive oil, tomato paste, salt and 4-5 tbsp pasta water. Cook on medium heat until bubbled.
5. Then toss with your pasta on high heat for 20-30 seconds.
6. Divide between plates. Add chantarelles on top.
7. Garnish with lingonberry jam pipping small dots around the plate.
8. Add fresh parsley or wood sorrel and serve.

*Chanterelles grow in the southern part of Sweden. They are hard to find, but can be located in coniferous forests or a mixed forest. The cap is smooth, delicate, and gold-orange with irregular, uneven edges that are thick, blunt, and taper down. Underneath the cap, the gills have forked ridges with blunt edges and these ridges run down the matching gold-orange, firm, thick, and solid stem.

**Juniper berries grow all over Sweden. They are usually found in areas exposed to the sun, for example heaths or pens. They are collected from small juniper trees or juniper bushes. It has needle-like leaves in whorls of three; the leaves are green, with a single white stomatal band on the inner surface. The berries are initially green, ripening in 18 months to purple-black with a blue waxy coating.

CASARECCE WITH CARAMELIZED PORCINI & BALSAMIC SAUCE

INGREDIENTS ———

Porcini	30 G
Balsamic Vinegar	1 DL
Tamarind Paste	1 TBSP
Agave Syrup	1 TBSP
Crushed Red Pepper	1/2 TSP
Garlic Cloves	2 LARGE
Red Onion	1 MEDIUM
Extra Virgin Olive Oil	3 TBSP
Salt	1/2 TSP
Fresh Rosemary	FOR GRANISH
Pomegranate	FOR SERVE

DIRECTIONS

1. Bring a large pot of water to a boil and cook pasta according to package instructions. Set some pasta water aside.

2. Add olive oil in a large skillet over high heat. Add the mushrooms and cook until they just begin to caramelize on the edges, about 5 minutes.

3. Add the garlic and onion, cook 30 seconds to 1 minute or until fragrant. Remove the mushrooms and garlic from the skillet and place on a plate.

4. To the same skillet, add the balsamic vinegar, olive oil, tamarind, agave and crushed red pepper flakes. Bring to a boil over medium high heat and cook for 5-8 minutes or until the balsamic reduces by about 1/3 and is sticky to touch.

5. Reduce the heat to low and stir in the pasta and mushrooms. Toss to coat, if the sauce seems too thick, thin it with a little of the pasta cooking water. Season to taste with salt and pepper.

6. Serve the pasta immediately, topped with fresh almond cream, rosemary, vegan cheese and pomegranate if desired.

NEW NORDIC MEETS OLD ITALIAN

LINGUINE WITH CHOCOLATE & BERRIES

INGREDIENTS ———————

Dark Chocolate	40 G
Blackberries	20 G
Bilberries	20 G
Strawberries	30 G
Balsamic Vinegar	1 TBSP
Coconut Sugar	2 TBSP
Coconut Cream	2 TBSP

DIRECTIONS

1. Place berries, coconut sugar and balsamic vinegar in a pot, cook on medium heat gently stirring mixture until the sugar has dissolved.

2. Bring to boil for 1 minutes. Then turn heat down to low and add vanilla. Simmer approx. 8-10 minutes until you get thick syrup.

3. Remove from the heat, set aside.

4. Cook your pasta al dente, set aside.

5. Using a bain marie, melt chocolate carrefully. When it is comletely melted, add 3-5 tbsp pasta water and 2 tbsp coconut cream and then on low heat for 20-30 seconds.

6. Toss chocolate with pasta, top with berry syrup.

7. Decorate with chocolate chips and viola flowers, drizzle coconut cream if desired. Serve immediately!

FOR 200 G PASTA

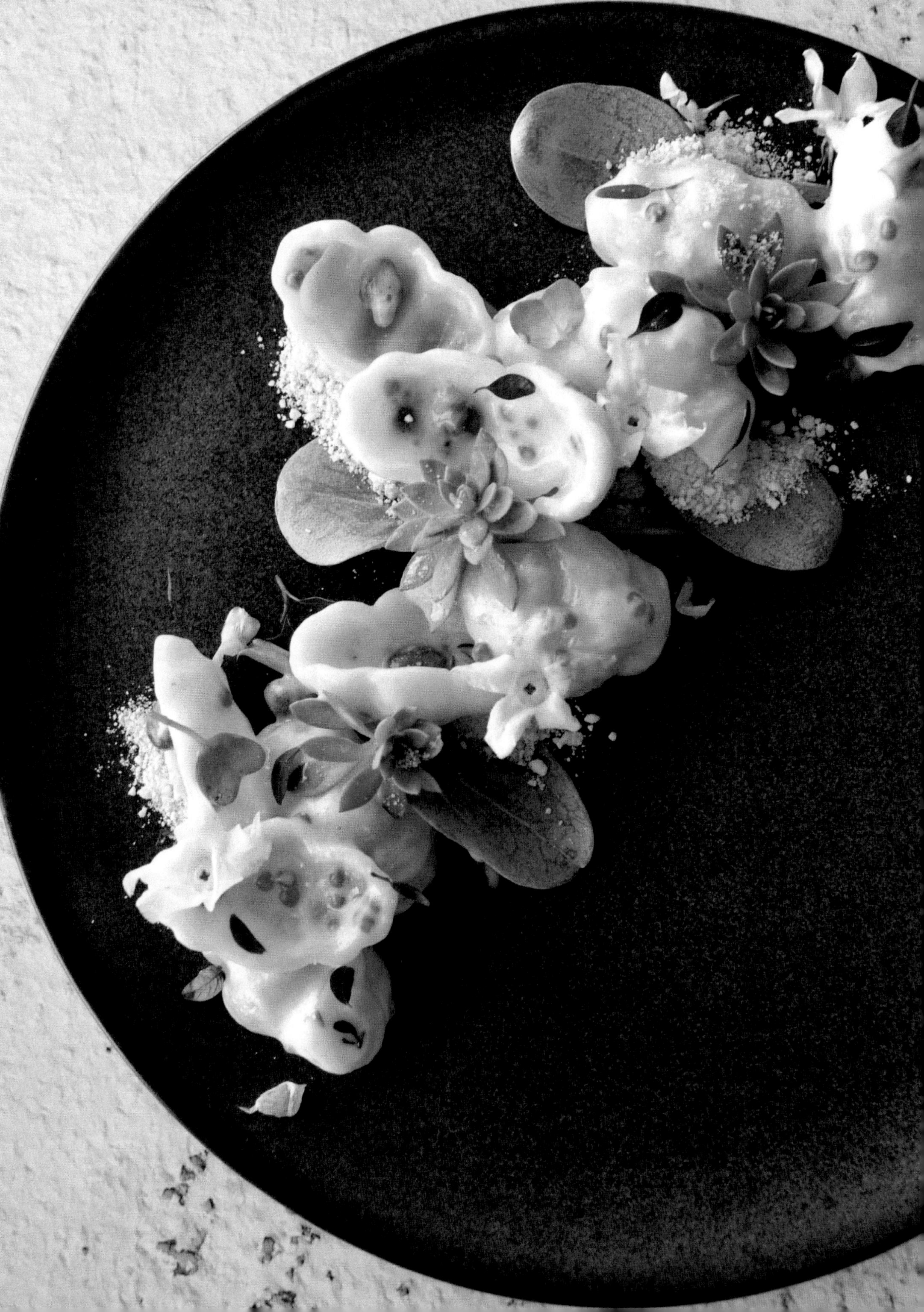

GNOCCHI WITH SKAGENRORA

In Sweden, Skagenröra is a traditional seafood . The name of the specialty came from a fishing port in the northern part of Denmark. Since World War II, it has been a Swedish culinary tradition for special occasions. The original recipe is made with shrimp and caviar but I have swapped these out for salted firm oat tofu and seaweed caviar to keep the same textures while keeping things vegan. It's a creamy salad with fresh dill and lemon so it's a nice marriage between more heavy foods like mayonnaise and fresh and light flavours. Think the pasta with yogurt. This recipe is a cold pasta sauce. You can combine with the pasta or you can top it on crispy bread.

INGREDIENTS ────────

Oat Tofu (or Soy Tofu)	250 G
Onion Chives chopped	1 MEDIUM
Fresh Dill	1/4 BUNCH
Seaweed Caviar	50 G
Nori Seaweed Crinkles	1 TBSP
Lemon Juice	1 TBSP
Vegan Mayonaisse	1/2 CUP
Vegan Creme Fraiche	1/2 CUP
Salt & Pepper	TO TASTE
Oyster Leaves, White Viola Flower,	TO GARNISH
Gangnam Tops, Daikon Cress	
Capers & Vegan Parmesan Powder	

DIRECTIONS

1. Crumble your oat tofu (or alternatively you can use soy tofu) using a forkinto a mixing bowl. If you want the pieces to be reminiscent of shrimp so make them quite small but make sure there's still some chewy texture. If you like smooth texture then process in the blender with a little amount of water.

2. Add your chopped onion to the bowl as well as a generous amount of salt and mix. We want to salt the tofu in order to get sea flavour in this recipe.

3. Then add the remaining ingredients, season with black pepper and more salt if want and mix well to combine. If you want you can leave the skagenröra in the fridge for a few hours or over night to allow the flavours to marry well or toss with pasta immediately, serve fresh dill.

NEW NORDIC MEETS OLD ITALIAN

CHRISTMAS EVE TAGLIATELLE
WITH CHESTNUT & OYSTER MUSHROOMS

INGREDIENTS ————

Oyster Mushrooms	250 G
Chestnuts chopped	100 G
Cranberry	2 TBSP
Coconut Cream	200 ML
Olive Oil	1 TBSP
Garlic Cloves chopped	2 MEDIUM
Shallots chopped	3 SMALL
Salt	1 TSP
Vegan Parmesan	4 TBSP
Fresh Parsley	FOR GRANISH
Nutmeg	FOR SERVE

DIRECTIONS

1. Heat the olive oil in a pan over a high heat, add the mushrooms, season generously and saute until deep golden and the liquid has evaporated. Add the cooked and chopped chestnuts and cranberries fry for a minute or two, set aside.

2. In a large pot, sautee the garlic and shallots with olive oil for a couple of minutes, until no longer raw. Add the coconut milk and bring to a boil. Simmer for 2-3 minutes. Then add the parmesan cheese, salt and pepper to taste. If your sauce is too thick, add some more milk or pasta water until it thins to your desired consistency.

3. To assemble everything, toss the pasta into the sauce, and add about 1/4 cup of the starchy pasta water to loosen everything. Stir in the mushrooms , chestnuts and cranberries, taste once more and make any final salt and pepper adjustments, sprinkle freshly grounded nutmeg and parsley. Serve immediately.

Tip: Other things that are great with these: wilted spinach, arugula salad, capers, lingonberries, truffle oil, toasted pine nuts.

ONE'S KNOWLEDGE MAKES THE WORLD MEANINGFUL, AND THIS MEANINGFULNESS COMPELS ONE TO PROTECT AND PRESERVE THE LARGER SYSTEM OF WHICH WE ARE PART.

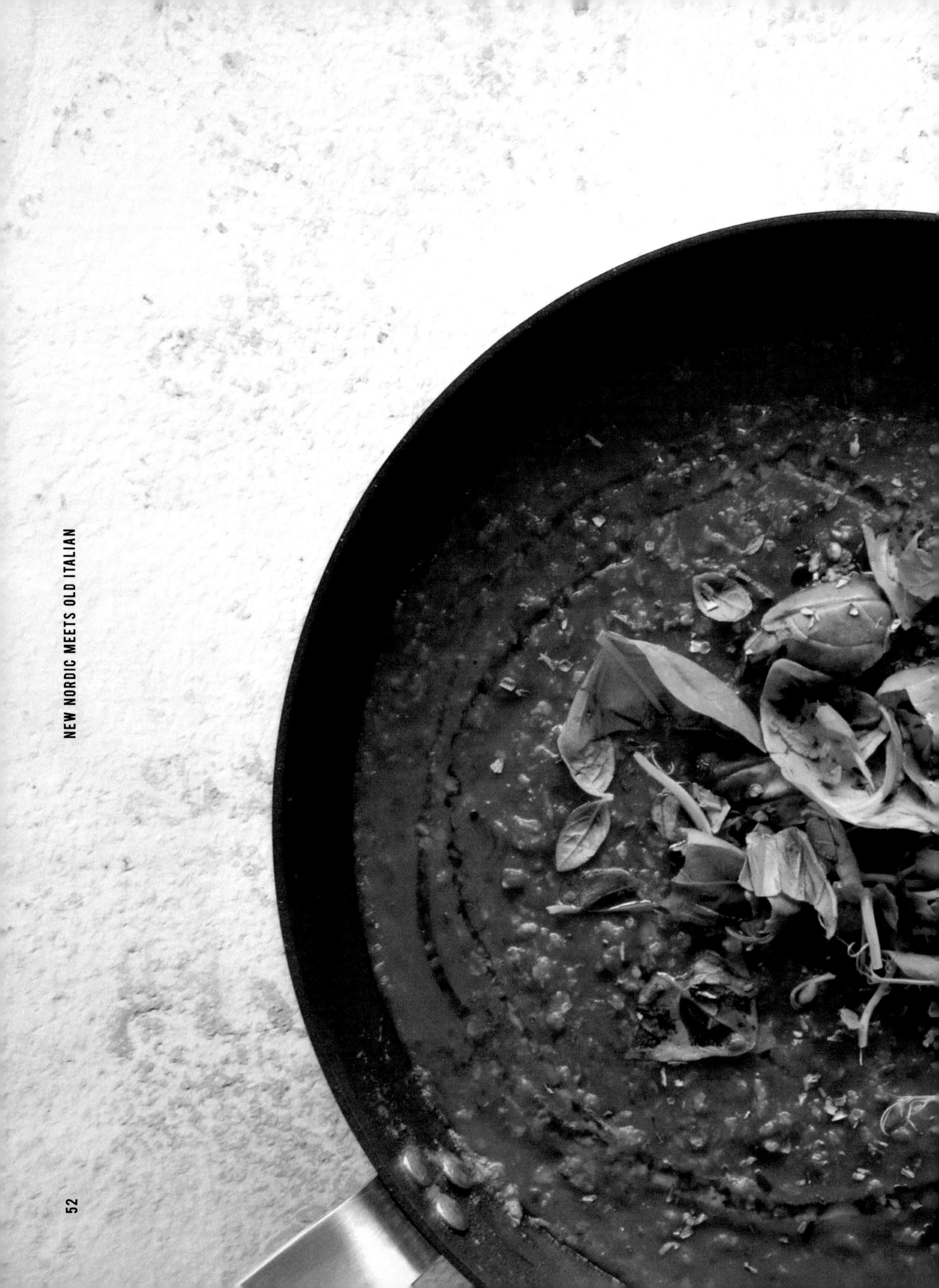

RED SAUCES

SPAGHETTI WITH HABANERO SAUCE

INGREDIENTS

Carrot	1 LARGE
Porcini or Veg Stock	1/4 CUP
Garlic	1 TSP
Onion	1 SMALL
Chili Powder	1/2 TSP
Olive Oil	2 TBSP
Sea Salt	1 TSP
Tomato Paste	1 TBSP
Red Bell Pepper	2 LARGE
Basil, Amaranth, Pea & Broccoli Microgreens, Hemp Hearts	TO SERVE

DIRECTIONS

1. Roast red bell pepper and carrot in the oven at 180° C until golden brown. Then remove from the oven let it cool for 15 minutes.

2. In a pan, heat a little olive oil, cut onion and garlic into small slices, add to pan. Cook until golden brown.

3. Then add garlic and onion into the blender, add roasted bell pepper and carrot. Add vegstock, olive oil, salt and chili. Blend well until you get smooth mixture.

4. Transfer sauce into pan, if it is too thick, add some pasta water. Cook on medium-high heat until bubbled and thick enough. Add one more tbsp olive oil if you need.

5. Add 2-3 tbsp sauce into a large and deep plate. Using a fork twirl spaghetti one serving inside of a soup ladle to get the perfect twist. Then, gently place it onto the plate.

6. Decorate with hemp hearts, fresh basil and microgreens if desired.

FUSULLI ALLA PUTTANESCA

INGREDIENTS ———

Dark Purple Kalamata	1/2 CUP
Capers	3 TBSP
Canned Tomatoes	200 G
Tomato Paste	1 TBSP
Olive Oil	2-3 TBSP
Garlic Cloves chopped	3-4
Salt	1 TSP
Red Pepper	1 TSP
Vegan Parmesan	TO SERVE
Zallotti Blossom	TO DECORATE

DIRECTIONS

1. Cook garlic, red-pepper flakes in oil in a heavy skillet over medium-high heat, stirring occasionally, until fragrant and pale golden, about 2 minutes.

2. Add tomato purée to garlic oil along with olives and capers and simmer, stirring occasionally. Then reduce the heat until the mixture is simmering. Simmer very gently for 40-45 minutes, stirring regularly, until the sauce has thickened. Once the sauce has been cooking for 30 minutes, half-fill a large saucepan with pasta water.

3. When the pasta is cooked to your liking, reserve 3 tablespoons of the cooking water in a bowl, then drain the pasta in a colander and return it to the saucepan.

4. Add half of the sauce to the cooked pasta, then stir in the reserved cooking water. Continue to stir the mixture carefully until the pasta is coated in the sauce. Season, to taste.

5. To serve, transfer the pasta and sauce to a warmed serving dish, then pour over the remaining sauce. Drizzle over the remaining tablespoon of oil and garnish with the parsley, if using. Serve immediately. Sprinkle with zallotti blossom and vegan parmesan.

Tips: 1. Cooking the tomato sauce for the full 45 minutes really intesifies the flavours in it, so try not to rush this dish. If your sauce becomes too thick before the end of the cooking time, add a dash of boiling water and continue cooking.

2. Use any shaped pasta you like for this recipe - just make sure you keep the quantities the same.

3. For the plating, pour a tablespoon in the middle of the plate. Splash with the back of spoon. Repeat process if you need. Place a little pasta on the sauce. Sprinkle vegan parmesan and fresh basil flower.

NEW NORDIC MEETS OLD ITALIAN

SPAGHETTI WITH GRILLED GINGERLY TOMATO

The best pasta often starts with a simple base, pepped up with ingredients like chilli, parmesan and herbs. This pasta follows the model, but a little added ginger gives the dish an unexpected warmth and vibrancy.

INGREDIENTS ———

Tomatoes	300 G
Bay Leaf	1 LARGE
Garlic Cloves	1-2 LARGE
Fresh Ginger grated	10 G
Red Chili Pepper	1/4 TSP
Extra Virgin Olive Oil	3-4 TBSP
White Balsamic Vinegar	20 G
Vegan Parmesan	TO SERVE
Salt	TO TASTE
Nasturtium Leaves	TO DECORATE

DIRECTIONS

1. Start by dividing the tomatoes in half and removing the pulp and seeds in a bowl. To this juicy goodness, add olive oil, grated fresh ginger, minced garlic, fresh herbs, bay leaf sliced into thin strips, salt, pepper, and balsamic vinegar. Opt for a fresh bay leaf and white balsamic, but you can sub in your favorites with abandon. Smash ingredients with a spoon or fork to combine. Set aside.

2. Sprinkle the tomato halves with some salt and hit them with a little bit of olive oil. Grill tomatoes skin-side up over medium heat.

3. After about 10 minutes of cooking, flip them, add the pulpy mixture, and sprinkle those tomatoes with sugar to ensure sweetly balanced flavor. Cover the grill with the lid. Check on your tomatoes every few minutes to makes sure they are not burning. When they look the way you like 'em, remove, just let them cook slowly until they look exactly the way we like them. Check on your tomatoes every few minutes to makes sure they are not burning.

4. Meanwhile, cook pasta in a large saucepan of boiling salted water until al dente (8-10 minutes). Drain, reserving a little pasta water.

5. Add pasta to tomato sauce and toss to coat, adding a little reserved pasta water to loosen. Drizzle with extra virgin olive oil and serve topped with parmesan, and decorate with nasturtium leaves if desired.

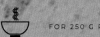

NEW NORDIC MEETS OLD ITALIAN

MAFALDINE WITH FENNEL CARROT CREAM & RED SHISO

INGREDIENTS ───────

Carrots	3 MEDIUM
Wine Tomatoes	250 G
Fennel Bulb sliced	1/2
Nutritional Yeast	2 TBSP
Garlic Cloves	3 LARGE
Extra Virgin Olive Oil	3 TBSP
Salt	2 TSP
Red Shiso	FOR GRANISH
Red Nasturtium Flowers	FOR GRANISH
Red Chili Flakes	FOR SERVE

DIRECTIONS

1. Preheat your oven to 200° C. Line a sheet pan with parchment paper.

2. Arrange the tomatoes, carrots and fennel (set aside fennel leaves to decorate your plate) on the sheet pan and season with 1 teaspoon sea salt.

3. Drizzle them generously with olive oil, arrange in an even layer cut-side down so each piece touches the tray, and transfer to the oven.

4. Roast until the tomatoes are shriveled and have released their juices and the carrots are tender, about 30 minutes. Remove the tray from the oven.

5. Meanwhile, bring a large pot of salted water to boil. Cook the pasta according to package directions. Reserve 1 cup of starchy pasta water, then drain in a colander.

6. Transfer the vegetables to a high-powered blender, along with nutritional yeast, 1 cup pasta water, and blend until smooth, adding more water as necessary.

7. Divide pasta between bowls and garnish with red shiso, green leaves of fennel, red nasturtium flowers, red pepper flakes and olive oil. Serve immediately!

A super flavorful, creamy sauce without any added cream or thickener.

SPAGHETTI PUTTANESCA WITH ANCHOVY

ANCHOVY PASTE

100 ml. vegetable broth

1 tbsp light soy sauce

1 tbsp caper brine

1 tbsp shiitake powder

1 tsp worcestershire sauce

2 tbsp liquid from fermented tofu

1/2 tsp garlic powder

0.7 g. kombu

1 tbsp nutritional yeast

1 tbsp miso

3 bay leaves

2 tbsp olive oil

1. Bring all liquids, garlic, kombu, nutritional yeast, miso, and bay leaves to a light boil, reduce heat to simmer, cover and simmer for 5-6 minutes
2. Turn off heat and allow to rest, covered, for 20 minutes
3. Strain into blender, add remaining ingredients except for shiitake and blend until smooth
4. Return to pan and bring to a hard simmer while stirring, whisk or stir in shiitake powder until combined and simmer for about 2 minutes
5. Return to blender and puree until smoot, pour into clean, jars and allow to cool before placing in the fridge or freezer
6. It will keep in the fridge for at least 2 weeks, or in the freezer for up to a year

PUTTANESCA SAUCE

1/4 cup extra virgin olive oil

One 35-ounce can whole peeled Italian tomatoes with their juices, crushed by hand

3 garlic cloves

3 tbsp anchovy paste

1/4 tsp crushed red pepper

1 tbsp tomato paste

A pinch of coconut sugar

1 tbsp capers

1/4 cup green olives

Salt and freshly ground pepper

20 g.Fresh Basil

1. In a large saucepan, heat the oil. Add the garlic, anchovy sauce and crushed red pepper and cook over moderate heat, stirring occasionally, until golden, about 5 minutes.
2. Add the tomato paste and cook, stirring, for 1 minute. Add the canned tomatoes with their juices.
3. Stir in the sugar, basil, olives and capers. Season with salt and pepper and bring to a boil. Simmer the sauce over low heat, stirring occasionally, until it thickens and is reduced to 3 cups, about 30 minutes.
4. Season again with salt and pepper. Discard the basil sprigs and garlic.
5. Toss with your pasta. Decorate with fresh thyme and green olives if desired!

The sauce can be refrigerated for up to 3 days.

PENNE ALL' ARRABBIATA

INGREDIENTS ———

Garlic Cloves	3 LARGE
Olive Oil	4 TBSP
A Small Fresh Chili or Dried Flakes	1 TSP
San Marzano Tomatoes	400 G
Fresh Basil	20 G
Salt	1 TSP
Red Wine Vinegar	1/4 TSP (OPTIONAL)
Vegan Parmesan	FOR SERVE

DIRECTIONS

1. To begin, heat a tablespoon of olive oil on a low heat in a pan and gently soften the minced garlic. Take care, as this won't take long at all and you don't want any colour on the garlic or it will impart a bitter flavour into the sauce.

2. Add the chilli flakes to the oil, temper for 10 seconds, then add the tin of tomatoes.

3. Cook down over a low heat for 10–15 minutes until the sauce has thickened. Taste and add salt and a little red wine vinegar if necessary.

4. Cook the penne in a pan of heavily salted boiling water until al dante.

5. Once the pasta is cooked al dente, drain and add it to the sauce, tossing to make sure the pasta is evenly coated.

6. Serve straight away and garnish with fresh basil.

One of the simplest and most well-known pasta sauces, arrabbiata consists of just tomatoes, garlic and dried red chillies . The dish is said to hail from the Lazio, and is most commonly eaten with penne as the ridges and holes of the pasta hold the sauce particularly well. The name translates to 'angry', which refers to the spiciness of the sauce, but you can easily adjust the amount of chilli to your palate.

Whatever shape you use, taking it to al dente and then adding it the hot tomatoey pan and allowing the two to finish cooking together will encourage the sauce to really coat the pasta, rather than just sitting on top of it.

ORECCHIETTE WITH BEET CREAM & BURRATA

INGREDIENTS ————

Beetroot	150 G
Aquavit or Vodka	3 TBSP
Almond Flour	5 TBSP
Almond Milk	250 ML
Garlic Cloves	4 LARGE
Lemon Juice	3 TBSP
Pink Himalayan Salt	2 TSP
Extra Virgin Olive Oil	4 TBSP
Chili Pepper	FOR SERVE
Onion Chives & Thyme	FOR GARNISH
Vegan Buratta or Ricotta	FOR SERVE

DIRECTIONS

1. Peel a 300g beet using vegetable slicer. Wash well, drain and cut into four. Place in a bowl, drizzle 1 tbsp olive oil, 1 tbsp vodka and sprinkle 1 tsp pink himalayan salt. Massage well.

2. Line a parchment paper on a tray. Place beets on the tray. Pour the remaining liquid in the bowl over your beets.

3. Preheat oven to 200 °C. Roast beets in the oven until golden brown.

4. Warm a pan over medium heat. Add a little olive oil and and sauté garlic until soft for. Then add almond flour and stir for 30 seconds or so until golden brown. Be careful not to burn. Remove from heat.

5. Transfer sautéd garlic and almond into your blender. Add roasted beets, lemon juice, almond milk, remaining 3 tbsp olive oil and 1 tsp salt.

6. Mix on high speed until you get smooth mixture. If it is not smooth enough, add a little bit almond milk or water and process again. I highly recommend to use blendtec wild side+ jar for soups and pasta sauces. It features an extra-wide base and a narrow fifth "wild" side that helps create a faster, smoother blend.

7. Cook your pasta according to package directions or your preference reserving a 1/4-1/2 cup of the cooking water before draining. We will use it to thin pasta sauce in case of need.

8. Pour the sauce in a large pot and cook for 1-2 minutes or until bubbled. If it is too thick, then add a little cooking water and heat. Then gently toss with your pasta to coat.

9. Garnish with minced fresh chives and black peppers. Top with vegan buratta or ricotta (see recipe in the cheese making chapter) if desired. Serve warm.

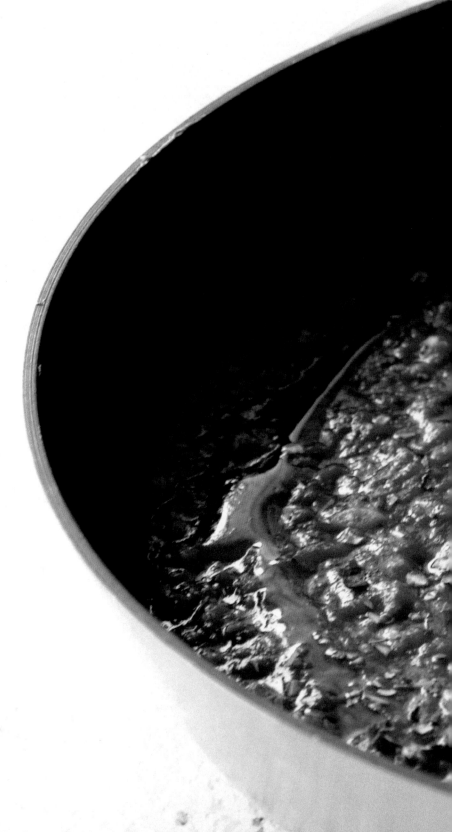

SPAGHETTI WITH PEA BOLOGNESE

SPAGHETTI WITH PEA BOLOGNESE

INGREDIENTS —————

Pea Protein Granules	30 G
Olive Oil	3-4 TBSP
Shallot	3 SMALL
Garlic Cloves minced	4-5
Tamari	1 TBSP
Tomato Paste	1 TBSP
Tomatoes	250 G
Coconut Sugar	1 TSP
Salt & Thyme, Chili	TO TASTE
Fresh Basil & Afilla Cress	A HANDFUL

DIRECTIONS

1. Place pea protein in a bowl, cover with warm water. Let it sit at least 15-20 minutes. Then strain excess water. Set aside.

2. In a large stockpot, saute garlic and onion until soft and fragrant in 2 tbsp. of olive oil, about 2 minutes.

3. Throw your pea protein in with the garlic, tamari, olive oil and coconut sugar until pea has been thoroughly cooked through, about 5 minutes. Season with 1/4 tsp thyme, 1/2 tsp salt and a pinch of chili.

4. Pour tomato paste, tomato puree and add about 1 cup pasta water. Stir to mix well.

5. Let mixture simmer, uncovered for 30 minutes. The longer the better, stirring occasionally.

6. Toss with al dente spaghetti. Decorate with sprouted peas and fresh basil. Serve with vegan parmesan if desired. Enjoy!

TAGLIATELLE ALLA VODKA

INGREDIENTS

Tomato Puree	250 G
Vodka	2 TBSP
Garlic Cloves	4-5
Extra Virgin Olive Oil	4 TBSP
Coconut Cream	3 TBSP
Vegan Parmesan	2 TBSP
Fresh Parsley	1/2 BUNCH
Salt	1 TSP
Sakura & Afilla Cress	TO SERVE

DIRECTIONS

1. Heat the olive oil over medium to med-high heat in a large, deep sauté pan, then add the chopped garlic.
2. When the garlic just starts to brown, add the chopped parsley, and turn the burner up to high. After a minute or so (when the pan is very hot), add the tomato puree and have the lid ready in case it bubbles out of the pan, then stir quickly with a wooden spoon.
3. Add salt and continue to stir often, making sure it doesn't dry up.
4. After approximately 7 or 8 minutes, when the sauce has started to thicken, check for salt, then add the vodka and stir well.
5. Add the cream, and stir well. Once it comes to a simmer, turn off the heat.
6. Stir in the chopped basil.
7. When the pasta is al dente, drain it in a colander, but reserve some pasta water. Add the pasta to the vodka sauce and stir well.
8. I love to serve it from the pot, and add a little sauce to each plate. If you are serving to guests, prepare a large pasta bowl, by warming it with very hot water, then add the pasta with sauce, and top with more sauce and microgreens.

A swedish way to eat pasta: "Serve it with ketchup!"

Anyone from Sweden will understand this topic without the explanation but let me pretext for anyone else. Swedes love ketchup. Seriously. Now, a lot of people will think this is weird, some will think it makes sense. After all, it is tomatoes. And, fries and burgers get ketchup so why not a different version of potatoes and meat? A good point, but not one that many will easily accept. Swedes are known for this eating habit and are proud of the oddity, yes, they know its not the most common way to eat pasta. :)

PENNE WITH PURPLE CABBAGE & BALSAMIC ROASTED ONION

PURPLE CABBAGE ⎯⎯⎯

Red Cabbage	250 G
Lemon Juice	3 TBSP
Olive Oil	2-3 TBSP
Salt	1/2 TSP
Pepper	TO TASTE
Pasta Water	1/4 CUP

BALSAMIC ONIONS ⎯⎯⎯

Agave Syrup	2 TBSP
Red Onion	1 LARGE
Balsamic Vinegar	2 TBSP
Olive Oil	2-3 TBSP
Salt	1/2 TSP
Pepper	TO TASTE

DIRECTIONS

1. To make cabbage sauce, juice a medium head red cabbage, place juice in a deep pot. Add olive oil, pasta water and salt. Bring to boil until thicken enough. Set aside 1 tbsp sauce to decorate your plate if desired.

2. Toss with your pasta until the pasta is coated with the sauce well.

3. To make balsamic onions, pre heat oven to 210°C. Peel the onions, making sure to leave the root ends intact. Slice the onions in half lengthwise, right through the root end. Cut each half into 1 1/4" slices, cutting again through the root end so that the layers of the onions stay together.

4. Place the onion slices in the roasting pan. Drizzle with the balsamic and olive oil. Sprinkle with the salt and pepper. Carefully toss with your fingers until the slices are well coated with the oil and spread in a single layer. Cover the pan tightly with aluminum foil and bake for 15 minutes until the onions are tender. Remove the foil. Carefully turn the onion slices over. Return to oven and bake uncovered for 15 to 20 additional minutes, until the onions are golden-brown. Remove from the oven and transfer to a bowl.

5. To assemble, place balsamic roasted onions to the plate, add some pasta tossed with purple cabbage sauce.

6. Pour some balsamic vinegar (from the bowl you roasted onions) to the plate. Pour red cabbage sauce over the plate.

7. Decorte with sea fennel and lace tuile (see next page for tuile recipe) if desired. Sprinkle maldon salt. Serve immediately!

LACE TUILE

Refined Coconut Oil	2 TSP
Water	1/2 CUP
Oat Flour	1/2 TBSP
Salt	1 G

METHOD:

1. Add a generous amount of cooking oil to your frying pan and set the heat to medium low. You want enough oil to coat the bottom of the pan, plus a bit more, so that it begins to pool. I used a small frying pan and approximately 2 tsp of coconut oil.

2. Once the pan is hot, and just before the oil begins to really sizzle, pour (or squeeze) a thin layer of your mix into the pan. I highly recommend using a mesh splatter shield to avoid getting hit with hot oil.
Depending on the general shape and size you want, you can pour in a small circles worth or coat the entire bottom of the pan.

3. Allow the cookie to cool down for a few minutes in the pan before you attempt to remove it. Using a spatula, gently scrape up one edge and work your way under the cookie. It should lift up pretty easily, if not, you need more oil in the pan next time.

4. Transfer the cookie to a cooling rack (or plate) covered with paper towels to remove excess oil. Allow the cookie to cool completely, and then use as a fabulous garnish for plating.

Notes: The amount of oil and the temperature of the oil in the pan are critical.

Not enough oil and it will not bubble enough to create the hole-y appearance. It will also not come out of the pan easily, which will mean the cookie will tear when you try to remove it. On the other hand, too much oil and you'll have one greasy cookie. Also, if the pan is not heated enough, the oil will not bubble. If the pan is not heated evenly, the cookie will not cook evenly. Once you have a sense of these core components, you will be a tuile master.

HOW TO MAKE MARINARA FOR CANNING

Ingredients:

12 pounds ripe tomatoes

1/2 cup dried/dehydrated minced onion (provides a great flavor boost and is especially suited to canning for long-term storage)

6 cloves garlic, minced

1/4 cup extra virgin olive oil

3 tablespoons brown sugar

2 tablespoons sea salt

1 tablespoon dark balsamic vinegar

1 1/2 teaspoons dried rosemary

1 1/2 teaspoons dried oregano

1 1/2 teaspoons dried basil

1 1/2 teaspoons dried thyme

1 teaspoon crushed fennel

1/2 teaspoon dried ground sage

1/2 teaspoon freshly ground black pepper

2 bay leaves

Directions:

1. Select the best tomatoes you can find. The ideal tomatoes are ones that are very meaty with few seeds. Roma tomatoes fall into that category and are the most readily available and they, like other paste tomatoes like San Marzano's, develop the best flavor when cooked down into a sauce. That said, you can use whatever tomatoes you have available and if they're grown in your own garden so much the better.

2. Blanch the tomatoes for a minute in boiling water to loosen the skins. Peel the tomatoes and squeeze out and discard the seeds. Chop the tomatoes.

3. Place the tomatoes in a large pot with all the ingredients . Bring it to a boil, reduce the heat to low and simmer, uncovered, for 2 hours, stirring every once in a while. Adjust seasonings to taste. Discard the bay leaves.

4. Use an immersion blender or transfer to a blender and puree until desired consistency.

5. The sauce is ready but the flavor is even better after a day or two. You can either enjoy the sauce now, freeze it, or can it for future use.

6. To can the sauce: Place 1/4 teaspoon citric acid or 1 tablespoon bottled lemon juice in the bottom of each sterilized pint-sized jar (double the quantity for quart jars). Ladle the hot marinara sauce into the jars, leaving 1/2 inch headspace. Wipe the rims clean with a damp cloth. Screw on the clean lids and rims. Place the jars in a boiling water canner and process 35 minutes for pints and 40 minutes for quarts. Turn off the heat and let the jars sit for 5 minutes. Remove the jars and let sit undisturbed for 24 hours. Check the seals.

Stored in a dark, cool place the jars will keep for at least a year but for best flavor use within six months.

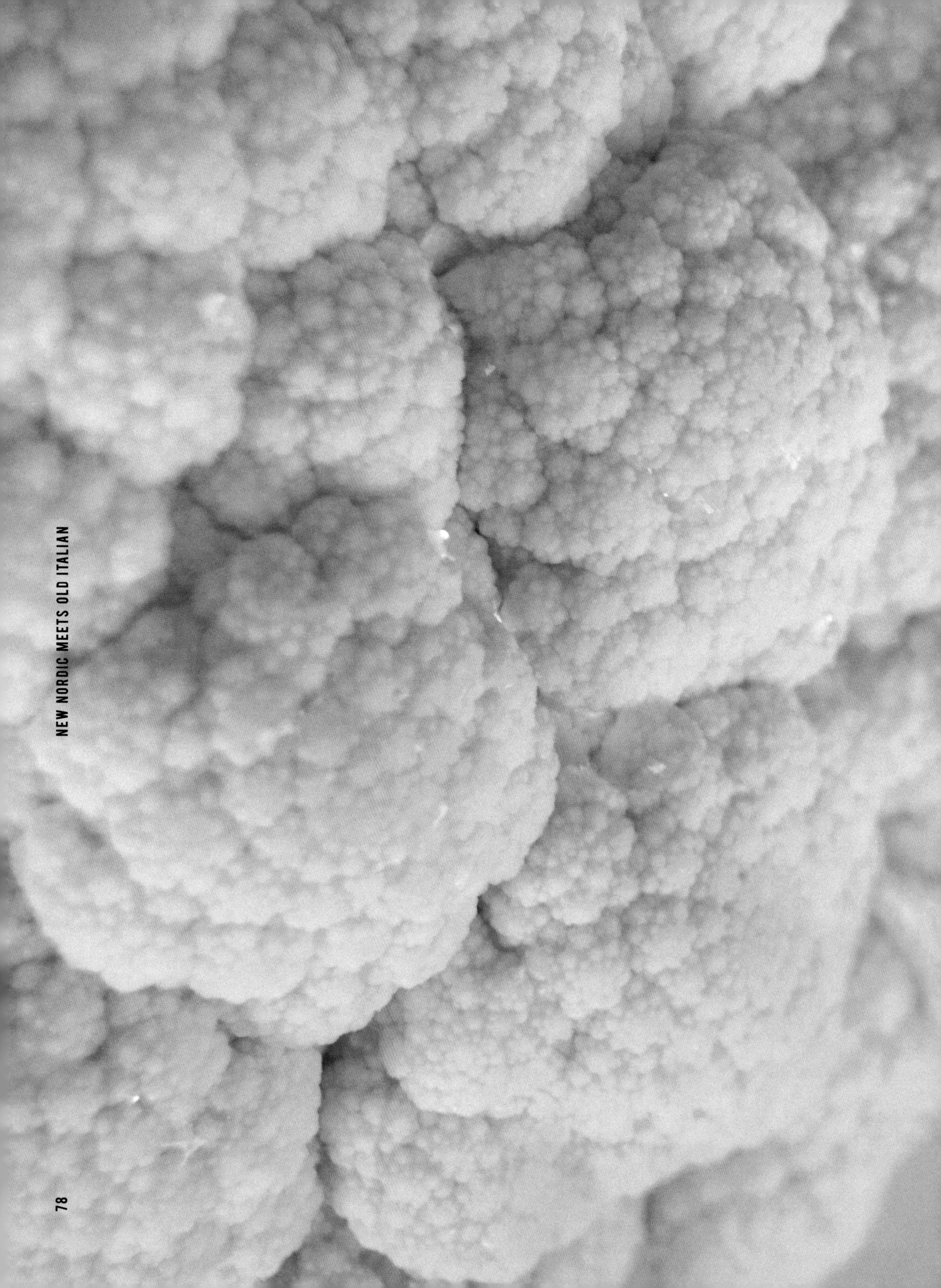

WHITE & CHEESE SAUCES

LINGUINE AL LIMONE E PEPE

RIGATONI WITH ASPARAGUS & GREEN ALMOND SALSA

CREAMY PENNE WITH MUSTARD GREENS, TARRAGON & MORELS

GNOCCHI PASTA WITH COCONUT CURRY

FETTUCCINE WITH HOKKAIDO AND SAGE

BUTTERNUT SQUASH - CAULI MUSHROOM LASAGNA

CREAMY CHIPOTLE FARFELLE

FUSILLI CARBONARA WITH TRUFFLE

PUMPKIN MAC 'N' CHEESE

PENNE WITH SAFFRON CREAM & PASSION FRUIT

CREAMY GNOCCHI WITH TARRAGON

FOR 250 G PASTA

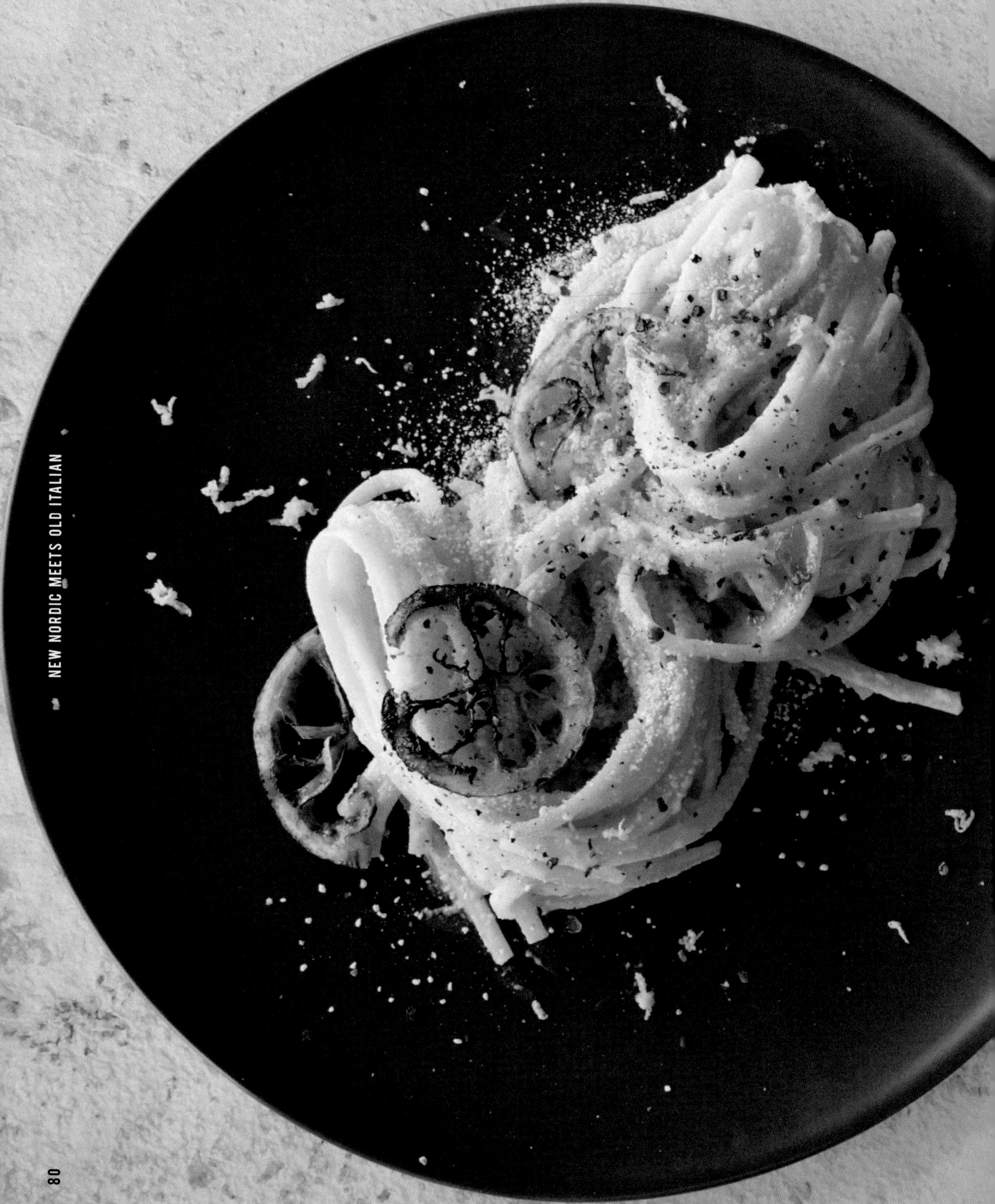

LINGUINE AL LIMONE E PEPPE

INGREDIENTS

Lemon Juice	3 TBSP
Bergamot Juice	2 TBSP
Bergamot & Lemon strips	8-10 SLICES
Coconut Cream	150 ML
Olive Oil	3 TBSP
Vegan Parmesan	5 TBSP
Ground Black Pepper	FOR SERVE

DIRECTIONS

1. Using a vegetable peeler, remove two 2inch-long strips of lemon zest. Thinly slice each strip lengthwise into thin strands; set aside for serving. Finely grate remaining zest into a large pot then add lemon juice, almond cream and olive oil into a pot and cook, stirring often, until softened and bottom of pot is browned in spots, 5–7 minutes.

2. Just before pasta is al dente, scoop out 2 cups pasta water. Add 1/2 cups from it to pan.

3. Cook whisking until each piece is incorporated before adding more, until the sauce is emulsified and creamy.

4. Then add your al dente pasta into pot.

5. Continue cooking by stirring often and adding 1 tbsp Parmesan a little at a time. Once all of the cheese is added, continue to cook, still stirring, until cheese is melted and sauce is creamy and clings to pasta, about 3 minutes.

6. Remove from heat and sprinkle with black pepper, toss once more.

7. Serve pasta topped with reserved lemon strips or toasted lemon slices and more vegan parmesan.

NEW NORDIC MEETS OLD ITALIAN

RIGATONI WITH ASPARAGUS & GREEN ALMOND SALSA

INGREDIENTS ———————

Green Almonds	1/2 CUP
Onion chopped	1 MEDIUM
Red Wine Vinegar	2 TBSP
Bay Leaves	1-2
Capers	2 TBSP
Fresh Parsley	1/4 BUNCH
Olive Oil	2 TBSP
Asparagus	1/2 BUNCH
Pepper and Salt	TO TASTE
Almond Milk	150 ML
Lemon Juice	2 TBSP

DIRECTIONS

1. Place almond cream and lemon juice in a pot. Add a little olive oil , bay leaves and 1/4 cup pasta water. Cook on low-medium heat until thicken. You can add a tablespoon tapioca to speed the process up. When it is done, toss with pasta well.

2. In a mixing bowl, toss the chopped onions ,green almonds and a pinch of salt with the red wine vinegar. Set aside to macerate for at least 15 minutes.

3. Next, add the capers, parsley and thyme to the bowl with the onions and green almonds. Slowly whisk in the olive oil. Add salt and pepper to taste. Set aside.

4. Heat a large skillet over a medium flame. When hot, add 1 tablespoon of olive oil. Add the asparagus, and saute until tender, about two to three minutes per side, depending on the thickness of the spears.

5. Divide the asparagus among pasta plates. Top generously with green almond salsa.

NEW NORDIC MEETS OLD ITALIAN

CREAMY PENNE WITH MUSTARD GREENS, TARRAGON & MORELS

INGREDIENTS ————

Wild Mustard Greens	100 G
Olive Oil	1 TBSP
Shallot	1 SMALL
Morels	30 G
Almond Milk	200 ML
Tarragon	1 TSP
Lemon Juice	3 TBSP
Nutritional Yeast	2 TBSP
Garlic Cloves minced	1 TSP
Djon Mustard	1 TBSP
Salt & Pepper	TO TASTE

DIRECTIONS

1. Bring a pot of salted water to a boil. Blanch the mustard greens for 30 seconds, then remove and shock in an ice bath to preserve their color. Drain the thoroughly and squeeze out any water, chop roughly and reserve.

2. In a medium saucepan over medium-low heat, add the olive oil. Add the shallots and garlic, and cook until fragrant, 5 to 10 minutes.

3. Raise the heat and add the morels, stirring frequently. Cook for 3 to 5 minutes.

4. Add almond milk and lower the heat so that the milk bubbles as it reduces. Cook for 10 to 15 minutes, until the milk has reduced by about half. Add the tarragon and nutritional yeast and lemon juice, stir for 10-15 seconds on high heat.

5. Serve in plates with the dusting of cracked pepper and vegan parmesan if desired.

NEW NORDIC MEETS OLD ITALIAN

GNOCCHI WITH COCONUT CURRY

INGREDIENTS

Coconut Milk	230 ML
Olive Oil	1 TBSP
Garlic Puree	1 TSP
Ginger Powder	1/4 TSP
Worcestershire or Soy sauce	2 TBSP
Carrot julienne sliced	50 G
Incaberries	6-7
Curry Powder	1 TSP
Shiitake or Porcini	100 G
Nutritional Yeast	1 TBSP
Vegstock	100 ML
Lemon Juice	1 TBSP
Red Pepper Flakes	1 TSP

DIRECTIONS

1. In a large pot, add olive oil and chopped mushrooms and garlic. Cook on high heat for 5-6 minutes or until crispy.

2. Then add coconut cream, curry, ginger powder, vegan worchestershire sauce, incaberries halved, carrots, lemon juice, vegstock, nutritional yeast and pepper. Cook on medium heat for about 15 minutes or until thicken.

3. Transfer your cooked pasta into pan, toss with sauce.

4. Garnish with incaberries, vegan parmesan and thyme if desired. Serve warm.

FETTUCCINE WITH HOKKAIDO AND SAGE

INGREDIENTS

Hokkaido Pumpkin	600 G
Nutritional Yeast	3 TBSP
Garlic minced	4 CLOVES
Fresh Sage	7-8 LEAVES
Pine Nuts	3 TBSP
White Wine	1 DL
Red Onion chopped	1 SMALL
Red Chili Flakes	1/2 TSP
Salt	1 TSP
Olive Oil	3 TBSP
Vegetable Broth	2 DL

DIRECTIONS

1. Bring a pot of salted water to the boil for the pasta.
2. In a little pot or pan heat up some olive oil. Fry the sage leaves for a few second each. Take up and place them on a piece of kitchen paper. Then toast pine nuts in the same pan until golden brown. Then transfer to kitchen paper.
3. Saute finely chopped onion and garlic in olive oil in a pot.
4. Add the diced hokkaido pumpkin and saute gently. Add chili flakes to taste. Add white wine and vegetable broth. Bring to boil.
5. Let cook until the pumpkin are tender.
6. Then transfer mixture into blender. Blend until smooth and silky. If too thick you can add a little bit of pasta water.
7. Salt and pepper to taste.
8. Drain the pasta, mix with the pumkin sauce and serve in warm deep plates.
9. Add toasted pine nuts, sage leaves and vegan parmesan cheese if desired.

This can seem being an od combination but the super delicious Hokkaido pumkin delivers wonderful flavours and distinct colours to this simple recipe.

BUTTERNUT-CAULI MUSHROOM LASAGNA

DIRECTIONS

1. Preheat oven to 200° C. Cut butternut squash into cubes, scoop out the seeds and place open side down on a parchment paper. Place sliced onion and garlic next to it and drizzle it with a little olive oil. Roast until fork tender, about 30-40 minutes. Let cool. You could do this a day before.
When it is done, transfer mixture into the blender, add rest of the ingredients for the butternut cheese sauce, blend until smooth. Transfer to a bowl.

2. Wash and boil the cauliflower in a large pot with water for 10 minutes until fork tender. Drain well before proceeding. Transfer the cauliflower to a high speed blender. Add the remaining ingredients and blend again. Transfer in a bowl, set aside.

3. In a large skillet, heat the oil . Add mushrooms and shallots and salt, and saute over medium heat, until the mushrooms release their liquid and begin to brown. Add the garlic, bay leaves and pepper. Cook until garlic is fragrant, about 2-3 more minutes, turn heat off. You could toss in some spinach at the end and wilt for extra nutrients. Taste and make sure the filling has enough salt and pepper.

4. Assemble the lasagna: Add 1 cup of the butternut puree and spread out into a thin layer over the pan. Top with 3 lasagna noodles. Add ½ of the cauliflower cheese sauce. and spread out evenly. Top with half of the cook mushrooms. Sprinkle with ½ cup grated vegan mozarella if you prefer.

5. Add 3 more lasagna sheets. Spread out the rest of the cauliflower cheese mixture as evenly as possible. Spoon half of the remaining butternut puree, erring on the side of less than half, so you have enough to cover the top (save at least 1 ¼ cups for the top.)

6. Add the remaining mushrooms and all the good bits (onions, garlic) and sprinkle some more vegan cheese. Place the final three sheets over the top. Lather with the remaining butternut puree and sprinkle with the rest of the cauliflower cheese You could assmeble this 1-2 days before baking.

7. Cover tightly with foil and bake in 200° C oven for 35 minutes.
Then uncover and continue baking 15-20 minutes until golden and bubbly. Cut into 6 servings.

8. Garnish with optional fresh herbs (sage or rosemary)

9. Lit a candle and play some music. Enjoy!

BUTTERNUT-CAULI MUSHROOM LASAGNA

BUTTERNUT SAUCE

Butternut Squash	3	CUPS
Nutritional Yeast	2	TBSP
Onion chopped	1	MEDIUM
Olive Oil	2	TBSP
Water	5	TBSP
Garlic Cloves	4	MEDIUM
Salt	1	TSP
Black Pepper		FOR SERVE

BUTTERNUT SAUCE

Dried Porcini	50	G
Olive Oil	2	TBSP
Onion chopped	1	MEDIUM
Garlic Cloves	4	SMALL
Tamari	1	TBSP
Salt	4	MEDIUM
Bay Leaves	2	FRESH
Baby Spinach	A	HANDFUL

CAULIFLOWER BECHAMEL

Cauliflower Florets	250	G
Nutritional Yeast	2	TBSP
Lemon Juice	1	TSP
Olive Oil	2	TBSP
Water	100	ML
Garlic Cloves	1	SMALL
Salt	1	TSP
Black Pepper	1/4	TSP

NEW NORDIC MEETS OLD ITALIAN

CREAMY CHIPOTLE FARFELLE

INGREDIENTS

Blanced Almonds**	1/2 CUP
Water	1 DL
Chipotle Powder	1/2 TSP
Garlic Cloves	2 SMALL
Roasted Tomatoes	1/2 CUP
Lemon Juice	1 TSP
Fresh Thyme	1 SPRING
Olive Oil	1 TBSP
Salt	1 TSP

DIRECTIONS

1. Place the almonds, almond milk, olive oil, water, chipotle, garlic clove, roasted tomato, and lemon juice in a blender and process until smooth. Season with salt and pepper.
2. Boil pasta according to the instructions on the box. Drain and place in a large bowl.
3. Transfer chipotle cream in a pot, add 2-3 tbsp pasta water and cook until bubbly.
4. Pour chipotle sauce over pasta and mix well on medium heat for 20-30 seconds.
5. Serve with fresh thyme immediately*.

* This sauce is best served immediately.

** Use cashews in the place of almonds if desired, then remove olive oil from the list. Cashews have more fat than almonds.

NEW NORDIC MEETS OLD ITALIAN

FUSILLI CARBONARA WITH TRUFFLE

INGREDIENTS

Raw Cashews soaked	70 G
GF Nutritional Yeast	4 TBSP
Garlic Cloves	2-3
Extra Virgin Olive Oil	4 TBSP
Salt	1 TSP
Vegan Parmesan	2 TBSP
Black Pepper	TO SERVE
Truffle mushroom	20 G
Filtered Water	1 CUP (+1/2 CUP AS NEEDED)
Vene Cress	TO DECORATE

DIRECTIONS

1. Add soaked and drained strained raw cashews in 1 cup water. Process in the blender until silky smooth consistency. If the mixture is too thick, then add more water.

2. Add all remaining ingredients except pasta and truffle in the food processor. Mix on high speed until smooth.

3. Then transfer mixture to a pan, heat at low until bubbling.

4. Transfer your cooked pasta into the sauce. Mix well.

5. Add extra parmesan and decorate with shredded truffled mushroom.

6. Sprinkle black pepper, add some vene cress leaves and serve immediately.

PUMPKIN MAC' N' CHEESE

INGREDIENTS ———

Pumpkin	250 G
Onion	1 MEDIUM
Garlic	4 CLOVES
Olive Oil	1 TBSP
Tapioca Starch	1 TBSP
Almond Milk	1 CUP
Sea Salt	1/2 TSP
Chopped Sage & Thyme	2 TBSP
Nutritional Yeast	3 TBSP
Red Pepper Flakes	1/4 TSP

DIRECTIONS

1. Using a sharp knife, cut the tops of your pumpkin off and then cut pumpkin in half. Use a sharp spoon or ice cream scoop to scrape out all the seeds and strings. Cut pumpkin into chunks.

2. Chop onion and garlic, add into a large pan with a tabplespoon olive oil. Cook until golden brown. Then add pumpkin chunks. Stir-fry for couple of minutes on medium heat. Then add almond milk, chopped sage and thyme. Cook on low heat until pumpkin is soften enough.

3. Transfer mixture into a high speed blender like Blendtec with wildside jar. Add tapioca, nutritional yeast, pepper and salt.

4. Blend on high until creamy and smooth. Then taste and adjust flavor as needed. Add more salt for saltiness, nutritional yeast for cheesiness, sage or thyme for herbiness, vegan parmesan cheese (optional) for depth of flavor, pumpkin pie spice for pumpkin flavor and warmth, or red pepper flake for spice.

5. To heat/thicken the sauce, pour into a rimmed skillet and heat over medium-low heat, whisking frequently until sauce is hot and slightly thickened - 3-4 minutes. If it gets too thick, thin with a bit more water or almond milk.

6. To serve, add cooked pasta to the sauce and toss to combine. Top with vegan parmesani pine nuts, thyme and fried sage if desired. Serve immediately!

NEW NORDIC MEETS OLD ITALIAN

PENNE WITH SAFFRON CREAM & PASSION FRUIT

INGREDIENTS

Oat Cream	200 G
Chopped Rosemary	A PINCH
Garlic minced	4 CLOVES
Passion Fruit	1 TBSP
Black Pepper	1/4 TSP
Extra Virgin Olive Oil	2 TBSP
Salt	1 TSP
Saffron	0.2 G

DIRECTIONS

1. In a small pot on low heat, add oat cream and saffron. Stir the sauce in order to help saffron diffuse into the cream.

2. In a large pan, add olive oil, garlic. Cook until soften. Then transfer saffron cream in the pan.
3. Add salt and black pepper, stir well.

4. Stir the mixture for a short period of time.

5. Turn off the heat and add fresh passion fruit. Mix thoroughly with pasta, sprinkle chopped rosemary and serve!

*Pair with brown rice or quinoa pasta for best results.

CREAMY GNOCCHI WITH TARRAGON

INGREDIENTS ———————

Coconut Milk	1/2 CUP
Celery Stalk chopped	1 LARGE
Cauliflower Florets	250 G
Garlic Cloves	2 MINCED
Shallots	3 SMALL
Extra Virgin Olive Oil	1/4 CUP
Salt	2 TSP
Lemon Juice	2 TBSP
Black Pepper & Sumac	1/2 TSP
Nutmeg	A PINCH
Fresh Tarragon minced	1 TBSP + MORE FOR SERVE

DIRECTIONS

1. In a large saucepan heat olive oil. Then add the chopped shallots, garlic, celery, and salt. Sauté over medium heat until the vegetables are softened, but not browned. This should take 5-7 minute.

2. Add in the cauliflower and coconut milk. Cover the vegetables with a lid to trap in the steam and sauté the vegetables, string every 5 minutes to prevent browning, until they are fork tender. This should take about 10-12 minutes.

3. Once the vegetables are softened, remove the mixture from the heat. Stir in the pepper, sumac, nutmeg, lemon juice. With a high speed blender, blend the mixture until smooth. (A immersion blender will also work well.) Stir in the tarragon.

4. In this stage add some pasta water for about 1/4 cup and mix well. . The mixture shouldn't be too thin or thick. If you need, add more water.

5. Transfer mixture in a skillet. Cook on low-medium heat stirring occasionaly until bubbled. Add extra olive oil if you need. I prefer to add 2 tbsp extra in order to make sauce more creamy and sticky.

6. Toss with pasta. Divide between plates.

7. Decorate with fresh tarragon, purple violet, scarlet and sakura cress if desired.

GREEN SAUCES

ORECCHIETTE WITH SPIRULINA MATCHA CREAM & OYSTER LEAF

SPAGHETTI WITH PURSLANE PESTO

PURPLE POTATO GNOCCHI WITH PESTO & ALMOND RICOTTA

FARFELLE WITH MATCHA CREAM, SEA FENNEL & MORELS

A GARDEN IN THE PLATE: RAW ZOODLES

UDON NOODLE WITH SHIITAKE, MISO & TOFU

SPAGHETTI WITH GINGER BROCCOLI SAUCE

WOOD SORREL AVOCADO PESTO

CREAMY BROAD BEAN PENNE WITH ARTICHOKE LEAF MEAT

RIGATONI WITH COURGETTE CREAM & TARRAGON PEARLS

BONUS RECIPE - CHANTERELLE PESTO

NEW NORDIC MEETS OLD ITALIAN

ORECCHIETTE WITH SPIRULINA MATCHA CREAM & OYSTER LEAF

INGREDIENTS

Avocado	1 RIPE
Cashews soaked	50 G
Matcha Powder	1 TSP
Spirulina Powder	1/2 TSP
Olive Oil	2-3 TBSP
Jalapeno chopped	1 TSP
Garlic Cloves minced	3-4
Shallots chopped	2-3
Himalayan Salt	1 TSP
Oyster Leaves	8-9
Vegan Parmesan	FOR SERVE
Scarlet Cress	FOR GARNISH
White Violet	FOR GARNISH
Gangnam Tops	FOR GARNISH

DIRECTIONS

1. In large nonstick skillet, heat oil over medium-high heat. When it shimmers, add onion and cook for 5 to 7 minutes, until softened. Add garlic and cook for about 1 minute more, until fragrant. Transfer mixture to blender, reserving skillet for later use. Add soaked cashews, 100ml pasta water, peeled avocado, matcha powder, lemon juice and salt. Blend on high speed for about 2 minutes, until very smooth.

2. Transfer mixture in a deep and wide pot. Cook on medium heat until bubbled. If the mixture is too thick, add some pasta water and olive oil.

3. Wash and dry your oyster leaves. Heat the skillet again add a little bit olive oil, transfer oyster leaves into the skillet. Fry until vibrant green. Sprinkle a bit salt. Remove from the heat. Set aside.

4. Over low heat, add sauce to pot of pasta and toss to coat, about 2 minutes, until heated through. Taste and adjust seasoning. Top each serving with fried oyster leaves and vegan parmesan. Garnish with white violet leaves, gangnam tops and scarlet cress if desired.

Tip: Other things that are great with these: cherry tomatoes, pine nuts, sesame seeds, onion chives, leeks, parsley.

SPAGHETTI WITH PURSLANE PESTO

INGREDIENTS ————

Purslane	120 G
Olive Oil	5-6 TBSP
Garlic Cloves minced	1-2
Sunflower Seeds	65 G
Lemon Juice	1
Salt & Pepper	TO TASTE
Pasta Water	170 ML
Vegan Parmesan	TO SERVE

DIRECTIONS

1. In a high speed blender, puree the purslane, sunflower seeds and garlic with the lemon juice until you get extra smooth mixture. Mix in the oil, season with salt.

2. Cook the spaghetti in boiling salted water until just al dente. Set aside approx. 170 ml of cooking water, drain the spaghetti.

3. Return the spaghetti to the pan, mix in the reserved cooking water and pesto, plate up.

4. Top with the purslane, cheese, chili and sunflower seeds.

PURPLE GNOCCHI WITH ALMOND RICOTTA & PESTO

GNOCCHI DOUGH ——————

Purple Potato	300 G
Buckwheat Flour	1/2 CUP
Nutmeg	A PINCH
Black Pepper	A PINCH
Garlic Cloves minced	2 SMALL
Salt	1 TSP

GARNISH ——————

Fresh Basil Leaves

Toasted Pine Nuts

PESTO SAUCE ——————

Fresh Basil	1 CUP
Pine Nuts	2 TBSP
Garlic Cloves	2 SMALL
Lemon Juice	2 TBSP
Olive Oil	2 TBSP
Salt	14 TSP

ALMOND R   A ——————

Blanced Almonds	1/2 CUP
Lemon Juice	2 TBSP
Salt	1/4 SMALL

DIRECTIONS

GNOCCHI DOUGH

1. Cook purple potato in the pot until soften well.

2. Mash them in a bowl and set aside to cool.

3. When the sweet potato has cooled completely, add oat flour, nutmeg, salt, black pepper and garlic. You want to add as little as possible otherwise the gnocchi will be tough and rubbery. Add just enough flour so you can work with the dough without it sticking everywhere.

4. Divide dough into two balls and roll out into long strips. Using a knife, cut them into half inch pieces. Press with the back of fork to give them a shape.

5. Cook gnocchi in boiling water for about 5 minutes, you'll know they're cooked when they pop up to the top.

PESTO SAUCE

1. To a food processor add the basil, nuts, garlic, lemon juice, and sea salt and blend on high until a loose paste forms.

2. Add olive oil a little at a time (streaming in while the machine is on if possible) and scrape down sides as needed. Then add 1 Tbsp (15 ml) water at a time until the desired consistency is reached - a thick but pourable sauce.

3. Taste and adjust flavor as needed, adding more nutritional yeast (optional) for cheesy flavor if you prefer, salt for overall flavor, nuts for nuttiness, garlic for bite / zing, or lemon juice for acidity.

ALMOND RICOTTA

1. Soak the blanched almonds in water overnight. Rinse and drain.

2. Place all the ingredients in a food processor add 4-5 tbsp water and pulse until creamy.

3. Transfer the cream cheese to a bowl and let the cheese chill in the fridge for at least 1 hour before using it to allow it to thicken a bit.

ASSEMBLE

1. Transfer the gnocchi into a hot pan with a good dash of olive oil and cook to achieve an evenly golden-brown finish.

2. Gently heat pesto sauce in a separate pan, take 4-5 tbsp from the sauce and set aside to decorate your plate. Stir gnocchi in the remaining sauce very gently. The sauce shouldn't be cover the vibrant purple color of the gnocchi.

3. Divide pesto sauce between plates making dots on the plate. Place gnocchi pieces on the pesto dots carefully. Pour small almond cream dots using a pipping bag on the plate. Decorate with fresh basil and toasted pine nuts. Serve!

FARFELLE WITH MATCHA CREAM, SEA FENNEL & MORELS

CREAM CHEESE ———

Cashews soaked	100 G
Oat Tofu (or Soy Tofu)	50 G
Lemon Juice	1 TBSP
Olive Oil	2 TBSP
Garlic Powder	1 TSP
Matcha Powder	1 TBSP
Nutritional Yeast	1 TBSP
Salt	1 TSP
Pasta Water	150 ML

FRIED MOREL ———

Morel Mushrooms	25 G
Tamari	1 TBSP
Olive Oil	2 TBSP

DECOATION ———

Sea Fennel fried	TO DECORATE
Pastina (Mini Star Pasta cooked)	25 G

DIRECTIONS

1. In a hot saute pan saute morel mushrooms without oil stirring constantly. It will get dryer every minute. When you have them crispy and golden brown add olive oil and tamari. Stir well on medium-high heat for 2-3 minutes. Adjust seasoning if desired.

2. Crumble the tofu into a food processor and add the rest of the ingredients. Process until the mixture is very smooth, stopping to scrape down the bowl when necessary.

3. In a pan, fry sea fennel with a little olive oil. Set aside.

4. Cook your pasta al dente. Toss with little olive oil. Divide between plates.

5. Serve matcha tofu cheese cream over pasta or on the side.

6. Decorate with sea fennel, and pastina.

NEW NORDIC MEETS OLD ITALIAN

A GARDEN IN THE PLATE - RAW ZOODLE

INGREDIENTS ————

Zucchini	3-4 MEDIUM
Green Olives	1/2 CUP
Cherry Tomatoes	1/2 CUP
Baby Spinach	1 CUP
Hemp Hearts	TO SERVE
Orange Violet	TO DECORATE

FOR THE SAUCE ————

Hass Type Avocado	1 RIPE
Garlic Cloves minced	2-3
Fresh Basil Leaves	5-6
Almond Milk	2 TBSP
Lemon Juice	2 TBSP
Salt	1 TSP

DIRECTIONS

1. Spiralize your zucchini with a spiralizer, set aside.

2. Chop spinach leaves into small pieces. Transfer into a bowl.

3. Add halved olives and cherry tomatoes. Set aside.

4. Add peeled avocado, minced garlic, almond milk, fresh basil, lemon juice and salt into the food processor.

5. Mix on high speed until you get a smooth mixture. If you need, add more almond milk o water to thin.

6. To assemble, pour dressing over zoodle, olives, tomatoes and spinach. Toss to coat.

7. Sprinkle hemp seeds, decorate with violet flower. Enjoy!

Tips: Make sure that the flesh is firm and the surface is free from significant defects like large indents.

Select large size zucchini for maximum yield, but not too much flesh. Zucchini is high in moisture content, so overly large zucchini has a lot of flesh and can be come soggier after preparing when not connected to the skin. Don't limit yourself; yellow summer squash and mexican squash work well too.

NEW NORDIC MEETS OLD ITALY

UDON NOODLE WITH MISO, SHIITAKE & TOFU

INGREDIENTS ———

MISO BROTH

Ginger Root	2 INCHES
Coconut Aminos*	2 TBSP
Kombu Powder	1 TSP
Water	5 CUPS
Miso Paste	1.5 TBSP
Lemon Juice	5 TBSP

FOR THE NOODLE

Onion Chives	2 TBSP
Udon Noodle	200 G
Shiitake Mushroom	200 G
Snow Peas	A HANDFUL
Firm Tofu	150 G
Coconut Aminos	3 TBSP
Olive Oil	3 TBSP
Sriracha	1 TSP
Kale Leaves	1/2 BUNCH
Black Sesame	TO SPRINKLE

For the Miso Broth:

In a large pot, combine the ginger, kombu powder and 6 cups boiling water. Let soak while you prepare the rest of the ingredients about 20 minutes. Carefully strain the stock, leaving behind any sand that may be hanging out on the bottom of the pan. Add half a cup of stock to the miso paste and mix in a high-speed blender until dissolved and smooth. Add the miso to the stock, and taste for salt, adding tamari and lime juice until you like the flavor.

For the Noodle:

Bring a large saucepan of lightly salted water to a boil. Add the noodles and cook, stirring frequently to prevent sticking, until the noodles are tender. Drain the noodles and rinse them in cool running water. If not using immediately, toss with a bit of oil to prevent sticking. Otherwise, divide the noodles between 4 large bowls and keep warm.

Tofu:

Heat a pan, add the tofu and drizzle with 1 tablespoon each of the olive and soy sauce. Add the Sriracha and toss to coat. Fry until crispy. Set aside.

Shiitake:

Meanwhile, place the shiitakes and snow peaas in a pan, toss with the remaining 2 tablespoons each olive oil and soy sauce. Fry until tender, tossing once or twice, about 10 minutes.

Assemble:

Heat the miso broth until steamy-hot but not simmering. Add the kale and cook just below a simmer until wilted and bright green.

Divide the noodles among 3 large bowls. Add the shiitakes, tofu, peas and onion chives. Pour the miso broth and kale over the bowls. Top with sesame seeds and serve!

---

*Use soy sauce or tamari in the place of coconut aminos if desired.

SPAGHETTI WITH GINGER & BROCCOLI

INGREDIENTS

Broccoli Florets	170 G
Fresh Ginger	1 TBSP
Leek	1 LARGE
Lemon Juice	3-4 TBSP
Garlic Cloves	2-3
Pasta Water	1/3 CUP
Olive Oil	3 TBSP
Salt	1 TSP
Broccoli Microgreens	TO DECORATE

DIRECTIONS

1. Preheat oven to 180° C. Remove broccoli florets from the stems and cut into small pieces. Peel the stems, discarding the outside, then dice stems and set aside. Toss with 1/2 tablespoon olive oil and spread into a single layer on a sheet tray. Roast until broccoli is tender and starting to brown, 20 to 25 minutes.

2. While the broccoli is roasting, heat olive oil over medium low in a medium stock pot. Add in chopped leeks. Cook for roughly 4 minutes then add in the ginger, cooking for one more minute. Stir in the broccoli stems followed by pasta water, lemon zest, juice, and salt. Bring to a boil, reduce to a simmer, and cook until stems are tender and roasted broccoli is done.

3. Add in the roasted broccoli, reserving a few smaller pieces for topping the pasta if desired. Transfer to a blender.

4. If soup is too thick, add enough pasta water and olive oil to thin it down to a good consistency. Blend well until smooth.

5. Transfer mixture into a pot, cook until bubbled.

6. Toss well with spaghetti.

7. Serve with broccoli , pea & shiso microgreens and violets if desired or top with reserved broccoli pieces and vegan parmesan.

NEW NORDIC MEETS OLD ITALIAN

WOOD SORREL AVOCADO PESTO

INGREDIENTS

Hass Type Avocado	200 G
Wood Sorrel	30 G
Vegan Parmesan	1/2 CUP
Toasted Pine Nuts	45 G
Garlic Cloves	3 LARGE
Extra Virgin Olive Oil	4 TBSP
Salt	1 TBSP
Lemon Juice	1 TSP
Nasturtium Leaf	FOR GRANISH
Black Pepper	FOR SERVE

DIRECTIONS

1. Peel your avocado. Wash your greens and drain. Then place the avocado, nuts, cheese, garlic, herbs and olive oil in a blender and blitz until you have a course pesto. Taste and season with salt, pepper and lemon juice.

2. Whisk together the 1/2 cup of pesto with the 1/4 cup of pasta water in a serving bowl until combined. add the pasta and toss until completely covered in the pesto.

3. Add more salt if necessary, top with fresh basil, pine nuts or vegan parmesan and nasturtium leaf, then serve while hot.

Wood sorrel pesto showcases the herb's tangy, acidic flavour in a sauce that takes minutes to make. The leaves are combined with the ingredients typically found in a standard basil pesto, which means it's perfect for stirring through pasta.

CREAMY BROAD BEAN PENNE
WITH ARTICHOKE LEAF MEAT

INGREDIENTS

Fresh Broad Beans	250 G
Artichoke with Leaves	2 HEAD
Lemon Juice	2-3 TBSP
Water	500 ML
Onion	1 LARGE
Garlic Cloves	3 -4
Carrot	1 LARGE
Olive Oil	1/3 CUP
Salt	2 TSP
Affilla Cress	TO DECORATE

DIRECTIONS

1. Clean and cut onion, garlic and carrots. Place in a large pot. Cook with a little olive oil for 5-6 minutes or until soften.

2. Clean artichoke leaves till you reach the heart. Then cut in half vertical, clean fuzzy center with a teaspoon. Keep them in lemon water until use to avoid getting darken.

3. Transfer artichoke leaves to the pot with water and other vegetables .Bring it to boil then simmer for 30-35 minutes.

4. Let it cool down for 20 minutes and strain through a fine strainer. Remove leaves and carrots. Now you have artichoke vegstock.

5. Peel the skin of the broad beans one by one. (can be done overnight)

6. Add artichoke hearts and the artichoke stock in a stock pot bring it to boil and simmer until artichokes are tender.

7. Add broad beans to the pot and cook until very soft. Be careful not to overcook them. Otherwise, they lose the bright green color. We want them bright and vibrant.

8. Blend them until smooth, adjust salt, oil and seasoning. Transfer to a pot, cook for 2-3 minutes on low- medium heat until bubbled.

9. When your penne is cooked, add 3-4 tbsp pasta water to the sauce and stir well. Toss with penne on high heat for 5-6 seconds. Transfer to the plates. Sprinkle some vegan parmesan powder if desired.

10. Using your hands peel soften artichoke leaves. You will have soft leaf meat when you peel them. Drizzle olive oil and sprinkle some salt and pepper. Top your pasta. Cut cooked carrots into small cubes, decorate your plate as in shown in the picture. You can finish with a touch of affilla cress and viola flower if desired.Enjoy!

RIGATONI WITH COURGETTE CREAM & TARRAGON PEARLS

EVERY SINGE SOUP HAS A POTENTIAL TO PASTA SAUCE.

NEW NORDIC MEETS OLD ITALIAN

RIGATONI WITH COURGETTE CREAM & TARRAGON PEARLS

COURGETTE CREAM

Courgette chopped	1 LARGE
Shallot chopped	3 SMALL
Garlic Cloves minced	2 LARGE
Olive Oil	2 TBSP
Lemon Juice	2 TBSP
Salt	1/2 TSP
Pepper	TO TASTE
Pasta Water	1/4 CUP

TARRAGON PEARLS

Fresh Tarragon	15 G
Olive Oil	300 ML
Agar Agar	1 G
Water	80 ML

DECORATION

Affilla Cress	2 TBSP
Silver Powder	TO DUST
Zallotti Blossom Leaves	TO DECORATE

DIRECTIONS

1. To make courgette cream;
Cook the garlic, onion and courgette on the skillet pan with olive oil until soft enough. Then remove from the heat transfer to a high speed blender and blend with the lemon juice, pepper, salt and pasta water. Transfer to the pot. Cook until bubbled. Taste it and season with salt and pepper if you need, then transfer to a piping bag.

2. To make tarragon pearls;
Put a saucepan with salted water on the oven and boil it. Clean the bunch of tarragon and wash the leaves well. Cook the leaves in boiling water for a few minutes and quickly pass them in ice water to keep the green color bright. Then blend the leaves with a blender adding a few drops of cold water to make it liquid. Once the cream is obtained, pour 1 g of agar agar per 80ml water, bring to a boil. In the meantime, put the oil to cool in the fridge in a narrow, tall container.
Get a syringe without a needle, pull the tarragon cream and drop it into the cold oil. When the drops touch the bottom of the container, they will have become perfect pearls.

3. Cook the pasta in plenty of water. Then drain it and continue cooking in the pan with a little olive oil. The pasta will release the starch and absorb all the olive oil. Stir in a sprinkling of vegan parmesan and a drizzle extra virgin olive oil.

4. Place rigatoni in the plate as shown in the photo. Place courgette cream in the middle of each rigatoni using the pipping pag.

5. Decorate with zallotti blossom leaves, affilla cress and tarragon pearls as shown in the picture. Finish by dusting silver powder. Serve!

BONUS RECIPE- CHANTERELLE PESTO

INGREDIENTS

Chanterelles	200 G
Pine Nuts	50 G
Extra Virgin Olive Oil	80 ML
Garlic Cloves	2-3 SMALL
Onion chopped	1 SMALL
Fresh Parsley chopped	1/2 BUNCH
Blackpepper	1/2 TSP
Salt	1 TSP

DIRECTIONS

1. Carefully clean the chanterelles until all dirt is removed. You can do this with a mushroom brush, a pastry brush or with damp kitchen paper.

2. Heat a frying pan over a medium heat. Add the pine nuts and cook, stirring continuously, for 2–3 minutes until just beginning to brown. Remove from the heat and leave to one side.

3. Heat 1 tablespoon of the olive oil in the frying pan over a high heat until hot. Add the onion and fry, stirring frequently, for 2-3 minutes, until softened. Reduce the heat, add the chanterelles and fry for a further 5 minutes, until tender. Remove from the pan and leave to one side for 10 minutes.

4. Put the mushrooms and onion into a blender or food processor. Add the toasted pine nuts, Parmesan, parsley, garlic and the remaining olive oil. Blend until smooth. Add salt and pepper to taste. Add a little more olive oil if the pesto is too stiff. When cold, transfer to clean jar and store in a fridge - it keeps for up to two weeks.

Serve with pasta or knäckebröd (swedish crispy bread.)

In Scandinavia, we are lucky that there is a law called allemansrätt, meaning 'every man's right' or 'freedom to roam', which means there are no trespassing laws. Paired with the fact that the Nordic countries have the perfect habitat for many yummy edible foods, there is a tradition to forage.

With foraging playing such a major part in Swedish culture there are many recipes that make use of free picking. There's something so special and refreshing about creating festive flavours that hasn't come from the supermarket shelves.

INDEX

NOTES

NEW NORDIC MEETS OLD ITALIAN

NOTES

_____

_____

_____

_____

_____

_____

_____

_____

_____

_____

_____

_____

_____

_____

NOTES

NEW NORDIC MEETS OLD ITALIAN

NOTES

Made in the USA
Middletown, DE
24 October 2020